hed by:
an Hale in respect of Keenan Outreach, Ltd. Houston, TX
eenanoutreach.org

THORN

Harnessing the Fi
Found in Your

Cop

ISB

All

No
elec
and
publ

Som
prote

Publ
Mor
www

This book is dedicated to the surviving 10+. For without you, she no longer exists

Table of Contents

PREFACE

When a child loses its mother at the age of 18 months, the psychological effects can be overwhelmingly challenging. I lost the woman who gave birth to me, my twin sister and eight other siblings. I am the 10th child and the youngest. I grew up not knowing a single thing about my mom, except that she was dead and that talking about her was sort of a taboo "punishable by law" or a "sin" in our household. Or at least that was the atmosphere created by my dad and his second wife, my new step-mother. My mom's death was not just a regular death. There was so much animosity and anger surrounding it, that every piece of her existence vanished from the face of the earth and so did her side of the family. These important things were forcefully ambushed from my life and my siblings, and unfortunately, we were the ones to suffer due to the decisions of the adults that were in our lives. I grew up in an atmosphere where intimidation and fear were used as tactics of control in the household. A beating came for anything possible, whether you were involved or not and I learned to live with hate in my heart for the people around me. I grew emotionless to survive day by day. I began to build a bulletproof wall to protect myself from it

1

all. Up until the day I graduated from high school, I was in survival mode; surviving the Hale (pronounced hell in this case) House is what I called it. It was no place for abandoned children. One by one as my older siblings got older, each graduating from high school, they would leave to not return either physically or mentally. Was I alone, yes. Was there a way out, not at all. My dad and his wife left us defenseless against them and the world. So what could we do or where could we go? Throughout this book, you will learn a little more about the place that I never called home. What you read is only a fraction of what it meant to deny your children the right to their childhood and the right to grieve the death of their mother. I am going to share with you a few short stories about my experience and how this book and passion came to life.

What's worse than negative affirmations being spoken into your life, you ask? Zero affirmations. Let me explain. Starting from the moment they are born, as parents you are to gift your children the most positive support you can. Tell them how beautiful they are. Tell them how smart they are, you can do it, keep going. You are enough and so on. Your child will grow to know and believe that the world is theirs and that there is nothing that can stop them. They will exhibit high self-worth. On the opposite end of the spectrum, you have parents who constantly belittle their children. Slow down eating all that food, you're gaining weight. You're ugly, stop talking so loud, you're never going to amount to anything. You're going to be just like your father, a dead beat. You're just like your mother, a nag. These children will have to fight for who they want to be. Some give in to the negativity that their parents have spoken into their lives and spend life with low self-worth. However, a child whose parent doesn't speak anything into their child's life will grow confused and lost with nothing to hold on to. A life of indecisiveness, questioning and stagnation. These children have no idea who they are or what to do. Without any sense of direction, they can grow to become naive and helpless, like prey to the wolves and very similar to those who have negativity spoken into their heads. For children, negative and zero affirmations are the worst. Unfortunately, my experience lends itself to the latter of the three. Nothing was spoken into my life. All I knew was that I was in the way and that I needed to figure out how to be less seen as a threat, or issue, as a child. I had no authentic guidance and no sense of who I was. Needless to say, the life I survived is one that I would never go back to. There is truth in that it contributed to the person that I am today, but that goes without saying. The fact is that I fought against everything that was meant to diminish me.

The Rose and Her Picture

There was only one picture of my mother that I had privy to seeing at an early age. It was the picture in her obituary. Further along in the book, I will share it with you. In the obituary, my dad wrote a poem for her entitled "I picked a rose."

"I Picked a Rose"

I picked a rose one day
The rose was most beautiful
The rose was full of life
The rose was my wife.
I cherished that rose
I loved that rose
I protected that rose
I honored that rose
I enjoyed that rose.
That rose blossomed
That rose loved
That rose loved everybody
That rose loved life
and that rose loved me.
So if you have a rose
Love her while you can.

I believe that poem signifies the true meaning of a rose. It's within this poem where I find the issues of life can be truly blissful. Reading this poem is where I began to see the heart in my dad that he never allowed to be shown. From the very first time I read it, my heart was able to be connected to the love of my mother. Who knew that one woman could have so much power.

The First Time I Acknowledged You

In fall 2012, I went through a series of eye-opening tests. I was in college and that particular semester was such a blur. All I remember was feeling like I was navigating another world. If I could describe it, I'd say it was almost like walking through an underground tunnel. One that was very dark with the feeling of something such as the boogie man lurking, me searching for the light in such a chaotic world.It was quite a semester. I remember one night in particular. I was sitting down and I met a man named Peay. As I stated before, this particular semester was somewhat of a blur, so I don't exactly remember where we were. (When I say my mind was far from this place, you have no idea). This man, Peay, seemed to notice that I was struggling and having problems (I guess it was that obvious). He asked me a few questions to get me to relax, like, "How's school going?" "How are your grades?" "Is everything ok?" You know simple things. Then he asked me, "What's your mom's name?" I immediately said "My step-mother's name is Lisa," without hesitation or any emotion at all. He abruptly stopped me in anger and said, "No No No No No, What is your MOMs name?" I was baffled, I didn't know what to say, I was so shocked and lost for words. Maybe I said something wrong. I asked him "What do you mean?" " You know, the woman that gave you birth," he said. I then said "My mom's name is Gail, but my..." He cut me off and said, "Never deny your mother." He was furious, to say the least, and I didn't quite know how to react because I had been conditioned and forced from an early age to call my dad's second wife, "mom" and to never speak of my birth mother after her death. So this was new to me as an adult. New enough to now begin recognizing my stepmother as "step-mom" but haven't reached the point to begin recognizing my birth mother as my "mom." I had never publicly acknowledged my mom as my mom. He was right. I had been denying my mother for so long to appease my father and step-mother to the point where if anyone would ask "what's your mom's name? I would say "Lisa," my step-mother's name, instead of my biological mother's name. It was second nature and I did not even have to think about it. My step-mother's name would go on all documents and any type of application such as school permission slips, scholarship forms, etc. Now I know there is a space for "guardians name" on these official documents, (which is where her name would go) but for a child who is being denied the right to grieve or even remember their deceased parent, this can cause long term effects. This train of thought and "de-conditioning" would continue throughout this semester of college. He later asked more questions where I shared a little bit of this information as well. Honestly, it made him sterner with his initial observation, only to say it one more time before leaving, "Never deny your mother." I will never forget this moment as that was exactly what I needed to open my eyes. It was truly the first time that acknowledged my mom, as "my mom," and felt found by her. For the first time, I was able to breathe. I felt a sense of peace rush over me knowing that I too have a family now.

Now on to You. Yes, You - My Muse.

In the short time of life that I have lived, I have realized that grief, if not handled properly, will have adverse effects. If not handled appropriately and promptly, those that look to you will be subject to a lifestyle that caters to unfinished business leading to complicated grief. This self-help read was created with a broken heart in mind. It is designed to assist you along the way and dares you to live again. For plenty of people, grief is believed to be an emotion that tends to be more suitable if you deal with it by yourself. We mask our true feelings every morning and night. Pretending to be strong, pretending that everything is ok, pretending that we are over it. We don't like to talk about the deceased for fear of either offending the other person or because we feel that by bringing it up we risk ripping off the scab of old wounds and bring to the surface the pain associated with losing a loved one. Think about the last time someone asked you about your deceased loved one and asked something similar to "How are you and Kayleigh doing, I haven't seen her in a while?" Then you have to say "Actually, My wife, Kayleigh, died a few months ago." Immediately they are shocked, and offer an apology similar to "I am so sorry." After, you say "Oh it's ok." Then conversation typically seems to take a turn. The other person likely feels that they have crossed some sort of line that they regret and it's clear that they feel awkward as they don't quite know how to handle hearing such news. Sometimes they wait for you to go into detail as they don't know if it's safe to talk about. These are genuine responses for those that may not have experienced a close death in their life or may have their grievances to deal with and that's ok. Not all people are comfortable speaking about death. Some people, when asked these questions don't know how to respond and are extremely sensitive when asked about their deceased loved one. Especially if it's from someone that doesn't share an intimate relationship with you. That's the purpose of this. To give people the courage to speak about their loved one and their death without feeling that they are compromising their emotional state by discussing it; to begin to healthily heal broken hearts; and to normalize conversations surrounding grief and the dead. This is what needs to happen. We have to condone open discussions surrounding grief and part of that is understanding how you feel and allowing yourself to feel. This process can no longer be put on the back burner while you suffer the effects not realizing that your dismissed grief is what is causing you turmoil.

Permission to Grieve, Anyone?

While reading this book I ask that you tune into your whole self and if you feel like crying, I want you to cry with everything in you. Let it out and let it go. For a long time, I believed that if I started to cry I wouldn't be able to control myself and that I wouldn't be able to stop. I somehow believed that crying was essentially adding to the sorrow and that the more I cried the more pain I would be in resulting in a never-ending battle. For a lot of people, this is exactly how they feel in some variation of this. That crying is some sort of demon that means them no good. A sign of weakness and God forbid you are vulnerable. First, permit yourself to shed a tear or two. It's ok. No one is judging you and if they are, ask yourself "Do I care?" If you do care ask, "Why do I care so much" and "What is caring about someone else's judgment going to do for you?" Take a deep dive into that question as you will be surprised at what you'll uncover. Your healing is far more important to me, as it should be to you too, where you shouldn't worry about what someone will think or say if they saw you crying. So I say let it go and release the struggle. The next thing I want you to do is to breathe. Take your time and breathe. I recently read an article that broke down an understanding of who we are as humans. Amongst other characteristics, it stated that we, as humans, tend to be very impatient. Meaning that we want most things now rather than later. It also stated that we are lazy. We'd rather not work for things or play the long wait game. We'd prefer instead to have things at our fingertips fastly and easily. Life isn't meant to be rushed. We are purposed for living to embrace every moment that life gives us. In retrospect to that, you will have to put all your efforts into achieving complete understanding and freedom. Some things won't make sense until you've had an opportunity to meditate on it to seek its applicability to your personal life. In the words of the late Aaliyah " If at first, you don't succeed, dust yourself off and try again." This will be an uphill trek. When you climb a mountain, it gets steeper and steeper. You'll get tired and possibly feel that you are short of breath due to the elevation changes and thinner air. I promise you that what you are feeling is true but you must be keen on every part of your body and your mental state. You can suffocate!! Take your time and breathe. You will find rest and peace knowing that you are giving yourself space for healing. Going at your own pace does not mean that you are losing. It ensures that you are learning and growing with each step. If you read something that doesn't quite make sense to you, feel free to read that sentence again. If you read something that touched you or resonated with you, read it again. This was meant specifically for you.

Have you created your safe space and time to be dedicated to this journey? If not let's start there. Identify somewhere in your home where it's just you and this book. In addition to that, commit to yourself that you will read every day until you reach completion. What time will you read each day? Ask yourself, who is supporting you in this journey? I want you to take your healing seriously and know that you are taking the right steps to your new life. So before you dive in, take a deep breath (pause and breathe here) and let's begin.

Someone call an ambulance! Get help! We need help over here! With hundreds of thousands of heartbeats racing to the unknown and unseen finish line, hundreds of eyes embracing an unwanted, unasked for cinema; multiple minds soaring as far as they could take them, a nightmare has just begun. On just another normal day, 35-year-old Lisa, an account executive at a local agency, has passed out at the office and her life is now at the mercy of her colleagues getting EMS to the site quick enough. Little did she and her colleges know, she had an enlarged heart and it was time.

"Mam, can you hear me?" "I have no response team."

"Mam, can you hear me? " If you can hear me, I want you to know that help is on the way."

"Oh god, what do we do?"

Hiyaa Doctor, I hope you have some good news for me! Exhausted and lethargic, trying to exert what little energy left in his body, Marcus Blain, a 53-year-old man, awaits his lab test results. "There is no easy way to say this but, the sharp pain that you have been experiencing is not a migraine. We have discovered a tumor in your brain." In his confusion, Marcus asks "What are you trying to say to Dr? Come on, spit it out!" "Unfortunately, you have cancer Mr. Blain and it looks like it is in the advanced stage. I am sorry! " Marcus' heart drops to a pit of despair. His body is like a car with no steering fluid. Too heavy to do any type of direct control to get back on track. His wife Maxine, by his side, began to weep. Tears so thick she is unable to see clearly. Her strong legs lose their way and she collapses to the floor. She knew it was his time.

"Are we there yet? Are we there yet? Are we there yet?" Rose, an overjoyed 7-year old who won't make it to her first visit to Disneyland said. She bugged her parents the entire car ride there. Those words will be the last her parents, Josh and Abigail, will hear for the rest of their lives. Those were the words she said when their car was struck by a drunk driver where Rose didn't survive. Those words will haunt them in their dreams and will haunt the love that they had for each other until no end. The face of the drunk driver, a murderer, and a selfish human being is the only thing their eyes can see, as he robbed them of their life and there was nothing that they could do. Yes, it was an accident, but it was time.

17 Year old Ara, a junior in high school… and the stories will continue.

Death is a fate with no discrimination of age, sex, race, or cultural background. It arrives in each of our lives through various outlets but one thing stands; it stings those left behind with no regret. The pain that is attached to the death of a loved one is inexplicably real and must be explored in a way that is healthy for that individual. Just as there are multiple ways in which a person may die, believe me, you, there are also many different ways a person could react in their grief. That's right, grief! It's ok to grieve and mourn the loss of your loved one and note that if someone has told you to "get over it, it has been long enough," I urge you not to heed to that type of word vomit. Before we move on, know that you must grant yourself the right to grieve. If you can't grant that to yourself then I, Morgan Hale, grant you all the rights to your grief, your emotions, your feelings and your thoughts. If you chose to slam a door or scream to the top of your lungs for release, then I grant you that right as well. That's what this book is about! Taking your grief, owning it and not letting it, or anyone, control your process. Some of you may feel that you have it all under control and if you do, I truly applaud you and your awareness. You've displayed a strength in your heart that allows you to keep moving through life living up to your greatest potential. To those of you who are in search of answers with a pain in your heart that just won't go away, I have good news for you, as there is hope and healing on the other side. I invite you to go on this journey with me as we learn what it means to grieve healthily. I will reference a lot of my personal experiences. This is done in part as I want to welcome you into my home and my heart. I too know the pain of losing a loved one and the being left to pick up the pieces.

As you see, I have named this book THORNS and if you remember from the preface, the entirety of the rose, holds great value in my life. Thorns are traditionally associated with roses. When a wedding occurs, you are likely to see a rose. At a child's dance recital, you are likely to see a rose being given. At graduation, you typically see someone getting a rose. Anniversaries, Valentine's Day and just about any other special event, someone will get roses. The same also goes for when a person dies. We typically purchase roses to put on the gravesite. Some may even debate that the rose is the most beautiful and fragrant flower they have ever seen or smelled. Traditionally, when we are given roses we always inevitably see the top (the bloom) as the only part of the flower. However, it should go without saying that a rose grows in a thorn bush which means it has thorns on its stem. During my time as a grief coach, which I will explain later on in the book, I often reference the whole rose. Referencing the thorns as the issues of life (you may interpret issues as you wish). As on the surface, we are as beautiful as we want to be but just as a rose has thorns, so do we as people when dealing with grief. Those thorns represent all the pain and suffering that you are suppressing that no one sees. It represents the love you "once" had as you now are cold-hearted. It represents the walls that you are building. It represents the sharp and deathly words that will spew out of your mouth at any given moment. Grief runs deep and being unable to deal with your thorns or emotions will cause further harm.

In this book, I will share with you how my world was taken from me and didn't even know it. I will share with you the suggested steps that you can take to capture your grief and how to explore it for the better.

To start, if you are searching for a deeper meaning in coping with your grief, it begins with one thing and unfortunately, that means that someone you love (I put love in present tense intentionally) has died. Death is something that I believe must be understood and explained in its most simplistic form for the human brain to grasp without over-analyzing. As emotional beings, we must come to accept death just as we accept life. When a woman becomes pregnant or when a family adopts a new child, the world is filled with such happiness. We (and yes, I include myself) welcome the news into our hearts with pride. In most cases, it's a hard expectation for couples to reproduce to continue the family legacy. If newly married couples take "too long," the family around them either knowingly or unknowingly places an unrealistic amount of pressure on them by saying, "give me a grandchild, I've been waiting long enough" or "When do you two plan to have a baby" (Now that they have only been married for two whole minutes). Now I am not saying that this is wrong to do to the ones you love, but I want you to understand that it's embedded in us to respond and welcome only positive things into our life as only the "good" helps us to grow. But what about death? This will be a hard pill to swallow, but just as mom and dad expect to have a grandchild, do we welcome death and the emotions accompanied by it with the same dignity and respect that life brings? Do we understand that we must live each day full of love and gratitude knowing that life and death do not discriminate? I don't believe that we should live in fear. I believe in living a life of freedom from our grief just as we have learned to live free in the life that is breathed into our bodies.

I hope that you will read this book and gain the necessary outlets and resources that you need to grieve both the life and death of your loved one. One without the other doesn't exist. We all grieve differently and there isn't a "12 step" guide that will cure you in your grief. If you are looking for a cure in this read, my friend, I have news for you. You're not going to find it here. And before you stop reading, allow me to explain why you won't find a cure. To look for a cure for grief means that it must be curable and that we, without a doubt, are ill. Let me tell you now that grief and more specifically, your grief, isn't a sickness. It's an emotion that you feel, which means that the power is within you to harness that emotion for the betterment of you. What you will find here are exercises that I use in my sessions, and exercises that others have found successful for them.

Have you ever asked the question, "What if" or my all-time favorite "Things would be different if said person was here." That's where a lot of people get stuck. As most of their time is spent questioning the truth of the matter in their current reality. These notions often put people in a trance, a barrel of regret not realizing that they are the ones digging a grave for themselves. I am here to tell you to put the shovel down. I see you have been working hard on digging this hole. You've worked up quite the sweat. Relax and breathe for the pain that you feel, is truly like none other. You may not know it but you worked up some stamina, and I'm almost certain that this took a lot out of you. You must be exhausted. It's time now that you rest. For even in physical training you must rest for the next workout. When you're ready let's begin to refill the hole that you have just dug. I know you are asking "Why would I refill the hole that I just dug?" This might sound crazy but just as you have taken from yourself, you must refill yourself. Put it back. Otherwise, you will walk through life with an empty hole inside you, actually making that two holes. You've lost your loved one and now you're losing yourself, but at what expense? The idea of coping with your grief is to help you fill the hole that you lost in your loved one, with your loved one. I'll say it simpler: Fill the hole in your heart with your loved one. That's right, keeping your loved one in your heart is what is needed to move forward in your grief. It's where they belong.

Once you face reality and it begins to set in, I am positive that you will be on your way to true hope and healing. Acceptance is the key here and that could be anything. You know deep down what you are facing in your life and how it's affecting you. It's largely important to take viable steps to a healthy new you, because guess what, you will never be the same after what you have experienced. None of us are. I hope that you will read this book and begin to live. You are not alone. I too am here right along with you. I will walk with you through this journey. Though I am not physically there with you, I ask that you allow this book to be the catalyst that links you and me together.

ATTENTION READER:

Before moving on, allow me to preface the information and text in this book to be general methods of coping with your grief. Everything in the text may or may not apply to your individual life. If you are finding that you did not or do not exhibit some of the grief reactions mentioned here please understand that it is ok and that you are not expected to exhibit all the same behaviors or seek the same questions and answers. Each person will be very different in their reaction and should understand that if you do not experience it there is no need for you to begin to experience it. If an exercise that is mentioned in the book is one that you don't have a hard time with, I say congratulations. I recommend that you still read that section of text to have an understanding and empathetic view towards others and their grief response. Your response to losing a loved one should be different. Happy reading!

CHAPTER I

UNDERSTANDING LIFE AND DEATH IN OUR GRIEF

According to the CDC, approximately 2.8 million people die each year. Of that, the top five, in order include Heart Disease, Cancer, Accidents (Unintentional Injuries), Chronic Lower respiratory diseases and stroke. With the sixth cause being Alzheimer's disease. Whew, that's quite a substantial amount of people who die each year. Just as there are 2.8 million people who die each year, in retrospect that means that there are at least 2.8 million people who are suffering from grief. This assumes that every person that died knew at least one person. When life has taken from you, I urge you to think about this number as it could be a life-saving truth to know that although you have just lost your loved one, that you are not alone in this world. Would you also believe me if I said that people also make it through their grief? That's right, they live. Some may go through hell and back and some may not but best believe that you too can overcome your grief. No matter what the cause of death is, the fact remains, someone has died. Although it has been proven that a healthy diet and regular exercise can extend the quality and length of life, when we lose a loved one, we are affected in a way that makes it seem that we will never be prepared for such an event. In the introduction, I mentioned that death does "have it out for you and your family." Keep that in the forefront of accepting the loss. With the notion and understanding of this premise, I pose the question. How exactly do you plan to pick up the pieces of your life knowing this information? Will you live every day giving 100% to your healing? Will you show gratitude? Will you forgive others, and yes even forgive yourself? On the contrary, will you allow your grief in death to control your manifestation in life? That's quite a lot to absorb. I know. Try not to think too much about it, because if you're like me everything must be thought through to the very last detail, and before I know it, half of my day has just flown by and I have nothing to show for it. You see, our thoughts can get in the way of ourselves, and all of a sudden we find ourselves with the shovel back in our hands re-digging the hole that we were trying to refill.

If you are having a tough time coming to terms with losing your loved one, one of the most important things that you can do to manage your grief is to understand the reality of loss from death and your relationship with it. Now, I am not an international philosopher that studied all over the world with all the "greats" as my mentors. I didn't spend three to five years in an isolated mountain in China, where there was no cellphone reception, drinking tea, to only awake every morning to do three hours of yoga and read every scroll or book that my "master" had. I imagine that it would be similar to the Kill Bill movie where The Bride spends months with a master where she trains in martial arts to get revenge on all those that have wronged her. I consider myself to be a regular Joe-shmoe, who had questions and went looking for answers via Barnes & noble, amazon books, studied Kastenbaum and searched the local library. Here is what I discovered. As simple as possible, the Merriam-Webster Dictionary defines death as a permanent cessation of all vital functions: the end of life. That's easily put in a nutshell. No need to go looking any further. The question that I believe haunts us after losing someone due to death is not necessarily "What is death", but the question that steals our present is "What now, how do I now live without this person in my life? It's the unknown that drives us as a species crazy. We know for certain what death is but for some, we become a little frazzled for a moment at the actualization of living life after this experience. In some cases, we ask ourselves "How can I do this alone? As you are unsure where to begin. You may have been dependent on this person for quite a lot of things in your life. Our emotions are focused on the right now and at that moment there is sudden sadness, numbness, pain, hurt, loneliness and even feelings of abandonment where deep down we know it's not true. We know we can move forward, but that question can paralyze us and stop us in our tracks.

"What am I supposed to do now that you're not here?" For all the over thinkers and worriers, this is perhaps one of the hardest questions that you will face. The sentence in itself is an open-ended question. Meaning that it is open for interpretation and for your imagination to work its wonders. We begin to create an infinite amount of scenarios in our mind of what could be, should be, how things will be and how we will react, only to bring us right back to the beginning over and over again. Now, your health is in jeopardy due to the amount of stress you have put on yourself. For a lot of people, "not knowing" isn't good enough and here is the reason. We cling to a strong sense of control. We want to control everything in our lives that directly affects "me." We don't want to look uneducated and in most cases, we want to be prepared for what's "about to happen." Think of the last time you had a high profile interview. You made sure to have your resume edited 1,000 times, you printed it on "fancy" paper and made multiple copies for the panel. Your suit was dry cleaned, starched and ready to go. You've been practicing your responses to potential questions and did major research on the company. After all, in your mind, you were going to nail this interview. It's time and you arrive at the office 30 mins prior and tell the receptionist, "I'm here for a 9:30a panel interview with Pam Smith." You are feeling the most confident you have ever felt in your life. They call your name and you extend for a firm handshake, good eye contact and a million-dollar smile. In the interview, you answer all their questions perfectly, your amazing personality lit the room and you believe that you were for sure going to get the job. A week goes by and you hear nothing, so you send a follow-up email. They respond with, "Thank you but we are going with a different candidate." Stunned by their decision, you respond with "Is there anything that I could have done better with, or may you give me a little feedback on how I may best prepare for such a position in the future?"

All of that prepping and for what, to not get the job. Was it all for nothing? No. In this case, we want the feedback to see how we might not be disappointed next time. We do a lot of preparing for events in our lives. In most cases, it's a good thing but understand that no matter how much we prepare, we will not be able to control the outcome 100%

of the time. Certain things are beyond our control. And in some cases, we must find a way to move forward if there is no answer available. Here is the thing, the hiring manager could very well be in a fast-paced environment where he or she would not be able to offer you feedback on your interview. So what do you do then? Will you harass them until you get an answer? Of course not, so don't harass yourself in your quest for answers in your grief. Just as in a job interview I'm sure the candidate was confident that the job belonged to him, but the reality is that the purpose of prepping is to control/ manipulate the decision/ situation in his favor. No matter how much we prepare for death, it still will have a massive impact on our lives, always. The test here is that you must now decide how much power to give to your grief and take an active role in this process. You can either decide that you will give up searching for the next job, or you can take the advice from the hiring manager to improve for the next interview and finally land a career. You can decide that you will allow the grief to overtake your emotions and your livelihood, continuing to drown yourself in your sorrow and pain in your, "what now?" Or you can decide that you will honor your loved one by deciding to mourn and healthily grieve their death by seeking additional help if needed. Reading this book, reading other books will help you understand that the, "how do I move forward" is a question that is open for interpretation and answered only by you. Give yourself the power to answer it with love, peace, openness and acceptance.

Life, a word with a definition. Here it is - The condition that distinguishes animals and plants from inorganic matter, including the capacity for growth, reproduction, functional activity and continual change preceding death; The existence of an individual human being or animal. Just as there are 2.8 million people that die each year, in contrast, the CDC reports approximately 3.8 million births a year. When life is brought into this world, we see an overwhelming amount of support and camaraderie for the family that is expecting, as it should be. We spend nine months anxiously awaiting the new bundle of joy. We stock up on diapers, wipes, clothing, etc. There are X amount of doctor appointments, prenatal care and all sorts of planning that will happen before the baby is born. The keyword here is, "expecting." Think about it. When couples announce their pregnancy, we generally say "We are expecting a baby." We know scientifically that it takes a baby approximately nine months to develop before it is ready to be delivered. In some cases, the "My baby was born early and it's fine", or "I went past my due date" sentences are true as well. I get it and I want you to know that I'm with you on that. You're not wrong. For the purpose I am trying to make, I like to think of it in the eyes of a baker. No one likes for their cake to come out of the oven too soon, and you don't want to leave it baking too late. We want that special soufflé to take the time it needs to bake properly to truly satisfy the sweet tooth that's been desperately itching for something good. Expectant couples and their families live knowing that they will welcome new life into this world.

Take a brief moment, did we, as a human race, have the same courtesy and privilege of knowing our loved one's nine-month expiration date? If we did, would it have made things better? Or would that be nine months of unbearable pain having to look your loved one in the eyes for 270 days, 6,480 hours, 388,880 minutes; 23,328,000 seconds to know that their time is coming and there is nothing you can do except begin preparing for their death. Could you imagine sitting your kids down to tell them "Kids, your mom will be leaving us in nine months?" She will be dead and you will no longer be able to see her." How about grandma, pop pop, dad, and the list goes on. That's a difficult time and I know some of you have had to have this talk, (keep reading you'll know how I know this), and I applaud you for being willing and open to discuss it. Preparing for death is important. It can help tremendously in your grieving process (thus another reason why this book is being written). However, unlike the birth of a brand new baby boy or girl, the sting is completely different. Now, in plenty of cases, the doctors can give an estimated death timeline for those that are terminally ill, and you know what, it doesn't matter because the pain will still be great. Some will begin to see that person as dead before they are and begin to withdraw. Yes, it's a thing that happens more often that you would like to believe. It's called anticipatory grief. It's not easy to accept death as we do life, and here's why. Referring back to the definition of life, life has an expectancy to grow and have continual change preceding death. We like to grow as a people and once we stop growing we will find ourselves in trouble. Ask yourself, am I stuck in my grief? How has my grief changed me? What work am I doing that warrants these changes? If you are having a hard time figuring that out, do a self-observation. Take a look at old photos to capture your memory and note your response to seeing them.

Life is created. 1st, physical life was created by your parents. They may also create a life for you in terms of your cultural norms. The values and morals they teach you, where you worship, who you socialize with, the neighborhood in which you live, the activities in which you take part in, education, etc. All of that is a part of the life that is created by your parents. When you come of age, typically around 17/18, you begin to challenge the life that was created for you and begin to create the life you want. Whether that's going to trade school, college, moving out or immersing yourself in a different culture, life will change for you. You will begin dating and going on adventures that are either similar to what your parents have taught you or they are very different. Either way, you are already creating life, in your life. This is something that you should continue to remind and say to yourself during your time of grief. Everything you do at any present moment adds to your life. No, this will not take away your grief completely, this will help you manage it and help to reinforce your goals and redirect your energy spent on grief. If I'm completely honest, you may say that to yourself one day, where you probably find that it just wasn't enough to get you through at the moment. That is ok. Live in the moment and recognize that you are loved and that the grief you feel is nothing but love. Pick up that next day as moments don't last forever. Take that moment, remember how you felt at that moment and draw on that for the next time so you may begin to speak life. I promise you're one step closer than you thought you were at that moment.

How do life and death compare? In some cases, some might say that they both are unfair and I can agree with that. A woman who can't have children vs a woman who might as well be Mother Theresa that she has so many children (I can say that because I'm one of 14 children). A woman who has beat cancer three times vs a man who couldn't beat it not even once. A child born into poverty vs a child born into a royal family. I get it, it's completely unfair. Understand this, life and death are governed by a different set of rules, unlike laws, that we will never be able to challenge or demolish. Although, yes, there is a movie called, "What Happened to Monday," where a controlling government tries to control the population by limiting families to having only one child. In the movie, the dad of quintuplet girls has to force his children to take one single identity to keep all of them alive. Yes, they did their best to control the population but they still had no control over who gives birth to who or deciding who they would deem as anatomically able to give life. It just doesn't work that way. They are opposing forces meant to draw upon a different set of emotions. Some might even say that they don't compare as they are completely different and on opposite sides of the spectrum. Traditionally, one brings about happy feelings and emotions while the other brings sadness and sorrow. I say to that, you are correct as well. Life and death were meant to complement each other in a supernatural way that bridges the world of imagination and reality. Once you understand this concept and open your eyes to the world around you, I am confident that your loved ones will show up all around you.

Here's the reality surrounding loss due to death and grief. When a person dies, it is factual that they are no longer physically with you. They are gone and are never coming back. Remember, death is defined as a permanent cessation of all vital functions. They may be physically gone, but they are still with you and all around you. They are with you in your thoughts, your actions and your memories. Your loved ones will show up in your family members and will sometimes show up in strangers if you are keen on it. They will show up when you need them the most and even when it feels like you are all alone. You have to pay attention to the details. Start by looking at the norms in your life that are now second nature where you do them without even noticing. Think about it. Why do you talk a certain way, why do you wear a certain color? Is it because your loved one told you at some point that you look beautiful in that color? We were meant to live a life that continues to love, although we have lost. In my first year of college, I had a 2004 black Saturn, a four-door sedan. At some point, I started looking for my next vehicle. I wanted something that I had not seen on the road before. I wanted to be different, let's just say a trendsetter. I didn't want anyone to have the same car as I did. After all of my research (meaning I looked at multiple cars on different websites) of finding the perfect car that nobody had (sounds silly right, unless I'm inventing the new car), I finally settled on wanting a red four-door Jeep Wrangler with a stick shift. Go ahead and laugh at me because, I know. I must have been crazy to think that I would be the only one with that kind of vehicle. Moreover, I got excited that I chose something so exclusive in my eyes. I told my twin sister, got her all excited, and even went to test drive one. I knew that this would be the vehicle of choice that **NOBODY** had. It was truly all I could think about. As time went on I found myself needing to drive outside of the campus, in my saturn, as typically I did not need to leave the university. That day as I was driving, I kid you not, I probably saw about 10 red jeeps which were far too many driving out on the streets to be exclusive, in my opinion. Every time I saw one I became even more excited because I was seeing my dream car, although I hadn't purchased mine yet. I thought to myself, "everyone has a jeep now that I want one," and I could not stop laughing at myself for thinking that! As if somehow all these people infiltrated my brain, saw that I wanted that specific car and took my idea. Had those jeeps always been there? Absolutely. Were people buying jeeps, far before I thought of it? Definitely. Why was I just now seeing them? That's because my eyes hadn't been open to the idea of having a Jeep until that time. I am sure that I have driven past them on multiple occasions but unfortunately, they were all a part of the everyday blur. The same concept applies to the death of a loved one. Don't obsess over it but they are in our everyday activities and you may miss them because we are busy trying to suppress how we feel and ignoring everything around us. When you slow down to accept what you're feeling and intentionally welcome the idea that, yes, they have passed away, but they are with you, I know you will find peace in your pain.

In understanding life and death as ones who are mourning and grieving, we sometimes focus on the bad, which I like to refer to as death. This is done unintentionally in our sub-conscience mind. Our thoughts turn against us in a way that we do not expect them to do. Our thoughts and pain become the death of us. We begin to do and say things that may not be true. We start to place blame on either ourselves or others and ultimately become prisoners of our doing. For reasons in which I don't want to get too far into here, there is a strong alliance in the fruition of the words you speak and the actions you take in your life.

On my journey to help as many people as possible to cope with the loss of a loved one, I created an organization called Keenan Outreach, Ltd. As a part of the mission, we facilitate small grief relief support groups where we tackle a different topic each week. In week two, we discuss life and death and how it relates to our individual lives. At some point during the discussion an exercise is facilitated in which we ask each participant to:

A.) say something that they believe is negative about themselves and then

B.) follow that up by identifying the positive in that negative, or positive period about themselves.

The goal here is to get participants to see that perspective is everything and that no matter what we must strive to speak life into our lives no matter how hard the situation may be. I am sure you have heard it before but the words we say have a massive impact on our psyche. We either believe that we are worthy or we simply aren't and the moment you begin to place blame on yourself. You have now deemed yourself as unworthy of that person's love. I want you to know that you are worthy. You may not have control over who dies and who lives but I guarantee that you have control over the things you say and do. Apart from this book, I want you to create a seperate journal to complete the exercises listed in this book. This is done purposefully as not only do I want you to read this book for understanding as I want you to take actual steps toward your healing. I told you before I will be with you through this journey of action so that you may activate your true self beyond grief, so, the very 1st exercise is called "A letter to you." This letter may be to whomever you want it to be; a friend, your mom, your dad, your sister, your deceased loved one, or even yourself. I only ask that it's a letter that speaks life into someone's life and that you end with a commitment. The reason why this letter could be written to anyone is that I have found personally that speaking life into someone else's life, in return helps the individual speaking it. Telling a person "You are such a beautiful person" or "Wow, You did an amazing job on this, I'm blown away" without any expectation in return is a direct positive affirmation to yourself. Because I want to be with you on this journey, I too have written: " A letter to you."

"My Dear Future Children,

I must be one blessed man for God to grant you to my care. I have a lot to tell you but I will keep it brief for now. I want you to know that when you came to this earth you were brought here with everything you need to be the amazing people you will become. There is no need for you to look anywhere else but within you. Dig deep for you know what to do. Attached to you is a purpose, a gift. Know that this gift is not meant for just you but it is meant for others. I don't know what that gift is just yet, but I will be with you every step of the way to assist you in uncovering your passion and purpose. I want you to know that there isn't anything that you cannot do. You will have to work hard and explore your curiosity to be all that you can. Life will be a challenge. Make no mistake this will not be a perfect road to travel and with everything in me, I will assure you that you don't travel alone. I can't lie to you, the thought of raising you all gives me a little anxiety. What if I mess up. What if you're sleeping next to me on the bed and I accidentally roll over on you, what if you one day decide that you no longer need me... what if! None of that matters, because guess what, I will do my best for you. I hope you know that I am not perfect, as no one is. However, I do believe that I am perfect for you, as your father. I want you to know that you are blessed. You are perfect for me, as my children. You are powerful beyond anything you could ever imagine. Take this time in your life to love unconditionally, forgive effortlessly, live life freely and unafraid. Love yourself 1st. I am proud of you for you are educated, beautiful and resilient. When I look at you, know that I see greatness and I will see that you live up to your greatness as your dad, but understand that you will have to find the strength within yourself to be greater than you were before. Continue to make me proud, but ultimately make yourself even more proud. I will never give up on you for you are my heart. I commit to you that I will love you with no strings attached and when the time comes I will first teach you how to fly and then we can fly together, and then one day I will watch you soar. I Love you with everything I have in me. - Your Dad"

Now that you have written the letter, I want you to keep this journal nearby as when you feel a little sad and your thoughts seem to cloud the way, read it as many times as you need to reopen the pathway. Understanding life and death plus the effects that it has on your life is largely important in beginning to cope with the loss of your loved one. We should expect death, but expect death in a way that allows you to live. It's not easy to expect it. When I say to expect death, know that I simply mean to accept it as a part of life, as that is the true connection between the two. Living completely free, fearless, loving with a mission to take every moment to cherish it. When you accept it, do not let it control you. Release the anxiety surrounding it.

In a long-shot the fear of death may leave some immobile day by day filled with emotions, unable to sleep with no ambition. Remember, it's not the "fear of death" that we are afraid of, it's the thought of not completely living. This fear of death is typically triggered by a turn of events, ie the death of your loved one. For me, this type of fear was triggered by an incident in 2014. I had just moved into my new apartment where I lived alone, and was completely absorbed in my career with no life. It was my first apartment. It was a motel studio-style complex where the front doors of each unit were visible to everyone who entered the complex. Needless to say, there was no private entry into my particular unit. Everyone knew who was in the courtyard and when you arrived home. The security to the complex wasn't the greatest and was on a busy street in a popular area near downtown. I was a little uneasy the first few nights and could barely sleep. I was kind of on watch throughout the night to make sure that I was safe. A little while later I became a little more relaxed and decided that rest was in my future for the night. I rested well until I was abruptly awakened from a deep sleep from what sounded like three gunshots. "Pop pop pop." As I heard what sounded like three gunshots, I wailed in terror and released three horrid screams almost like from the pits of hell. I believe my voice left me at that moment, followed by my soul. I had never experienced such a thing. I was 24 and had never heard the sound of a gunshot. While screaming to the top of my lungs, I immediately fell to the side of my bed in paralysis, laid on my back with my eyes wide and alert. With my heart pounding through my chest and my arms crossed over my chest. I remained in that position unable to move until I saw the sun come up and it was time for me to go to work. I was afraid to leave the apartment as I was sure I would see a dead body. I was afraid to watch the news as I'm sure it would be covered and was completely stressed the next day at work. My mind was racing, my sight was tarnished as fear began to rent a home in my heart. It had completely consumed me as I didn't know what to expect. I was afraid of dying and my life was over. That was my life for a long time. I would soon be freed from this nightmare but before, I would also be afraid to close my eyes at night because of "what if." I had never before gone through this and honestly didn't see any way to move forward. I had completely allowed my fear of dying to manipulate my reality. The reality was that it was a season in my life that needed to be tamed. I had a choice to either allow it to dictate my peace or I could decide that I wanted to live. Not only live, but I also wanted peace in all that I did.

As I stated before, life and death are phenomenons that will happen. Many people have lived before us and have died the same. Some choose to take life by the lap bar to ride the roller coaster. Some ride with their hands in the air, eyes wide open smiling and laughing, while others like to ride clenching to the safety bar, eyes shut and screaming for dear life "Let me off." You got on it, so go for the ride. Just as the roller coaster will have twists and turns and may flip you upside down, where you come out of it with "bedhead," I want you to think about this. You are actually on the ride. When we close our eyes and allow the fear to set in, we tell ourselves that we are the only ones on the ride or force ourselves to believe that since I am afraid everyone else on the ride must be afraid as well. You leaped and if you get afraid just look at the ones around you with their hands up enjoying the ride. Let that be your motivation to try and release the bar more and more as you "squeeze a peek" at them. Let that motivation birth within you.

CHAPTER II

THE SCAR THAT SEPARATES IMAGINATION AND REALITY

I Can Only, Imagine

S o you've made it to chapter two. I commend you and see, just like I said, defining death and life wasn't too bad after all. I hope it made you use your brainpower a little more during your time of grief. In your grief, have you ever imagined, better yet, created an imaginary realm where everything was perfect and that your loved one was still alive? Maybe the question of "what if" was too prominent in your mind that you decided to see it through. Is the pain of losing a loved one so great that you somehow forced yourself to create a world that's free of pain and suffering. You know, similar to the game SIMS or even fantasy football. Have you replayed the scene in your head multiple times to only change something so that your loved one would be alive? "Maybe if I would have double-checked the car seat, little Jason would be alive," or "If only I was there by your side at the hospital, I could have done something." Is it true that, just maybe, on Christmas, you went into a trance while making that secret family recipe? You started to reminisce by thinking "What would it be like at this moment in time?" Did you ever have a chance to meet or get to know your dad before he died where it left you to create his persona from shared stories and assumptions circling in your head? Here is your second of many exercises that you will complete. For this exercise, if you have ever asked yourself any of the questions above, I want you to identify one or two pivotal moments in your life and write the alternative to what you experienced. I want you to rewrite history. I want you to write down the story that you have told yourself countless times. What is this imaginary world that we create? I will answer that momentarily, but because I promised you that I would be there with you, so would you just indulge me just for a moment while you travel into a world with me? I will title this "If Mom was alive."

If Mom was alive - I would be surrounded by your patience and kindness. Although I have no memory of you I know and feel your love all around me. It was my first day of kindergarten. The sun was shining, you and dad made breakfast for the family. Instead of being disturbed by birds chirping in the window, as you walked into our room, we were awakened by your beautiful soprano operatic voice saying "Wake up my dear children. It's time to get ready for school. Come have breakfast with your mom. Today's a big day for you two." With smiles, we opened our eyes and were greeted with warm hugs and kisses. After we would do our morning hygiene ritual and meet you at the table to talk about what would happen today! We could smell the food from our room as the sweet aroma of vanilla filled the house. It was warm blueberry vanilla oatmeal with scrambled eggs, pan sausage and a homemade biscuit. What an amazing cook she is. It meant everything to my sister and me! We then went to school to meet our teachers. You walked us to our classes to meet the teachers as well. We visited my sister's class first and left her there. All seemed to be fine until I wasn't staying with my sister in the same classroom. Mom and I would take another journey to meet my teacher and a classroom full of children. Unfortunately, I wasn't the happiest. It resulted in me bursting in tears, crying hysterically. It hit me that I was being left there alone. I can see the hurt in your eyes and heart as you didn't want to leave us there as well. This was just as hard for you as it was me. You then pulled me to the side to hug and comfort me. This helped, but not much. So you stayed a little longer, but not too long as you knew that this would make me stronger. Guess what, it did and I lived. Further down the line, we would get older. My mom's patience and love would not run cold. Our residence would be in an amazing town with plenty of support and love from family. We would travel often, eat delicious food, take lots of pictures and have the most fun a family could have. All because you would be here. Later on in life, it was time for my twin and me to move out as we were going to college. I remember it like it was yesterday. You and dad helped us move in, along with our other siblings. We were your babies, the last of all the children to attend college and move. So this was hard for you. You tried your best to contain yourself as you helped us unpack all of our things into our new dormitory. When we got to the last box you purposely took twice as long to unpack it, only to begin to weep. Then before you knew it, my dad, my twin, you, and I were all hugging and crying as we didn't want to see you go as much as you didn't want to let us go either. Just like that, we all had dinner that night and while our older siblings went back to our hometown. Mom and dad stayed the night at a nearby hotel so that way in the morning we could have breakfast one last time and explore the campus together. The next goodbye wasn't as hard as the first one but still tough to handle. "I love you both." "I love you too!"

Is all of this true? Not at all. Did I create a realm where everything went as perfect as possible? Yes! Is this something that I wished to happen? Definitely! But whose plan did it go according to is the question? And is any plan perfect? The imaginary world we create is what we use to escape what we know to be true. We seek refuge in it. When it comes to grief some people obsess over rewriting what happened and this can have quite the effect on a grieving heart. For me, it was imagining a world where my mom was still alive and that my siblings and I were being raised by the two of them instead of my dad and my stepmother. It was imagining a world where love was unconditional and that we were raised to know that; In a place where fear and intimidation weren't the "rod" that raised us and to know that we were all more than enough. I imagined a world where being proud of your accomplishments was acceptable and that everyone was supportive of a true and genuine heart. How about you? Your imagination may look different than mine, as remember, I lacked the opportunity to know my mom as she died when I was an infant. As you see, I imagined a world with my mom being perfect. I will ask again, would this imaginary world be acceptable for those that are grieving? Here's the thing there is nothing wrong with a healthy imagination to escape the pain. A person grieving needs an escape. However, when you create this secondary realm, you must understand that it comes with risks. Normal mourning can become neurotic bereavement. In 2012, Stephen Diamond, Ph.D., wrote a study on the hysteria of grief. In the article, he mentions, amongst other points, two debilitating reactions; 1) Guilt about things other than actions taken or not taken by the survivor at the time of death and 2) hallucinatory experiences other than thinking that he or she hears the voice of, or transiently sees the image of, the deceased person. There was a third point in the study that referred to thoughts of death other than the survivor feeling that he or she would be better off dead or should have died with the deceased person. The imaginary world that you have created can either be your freedom to rehabilitate yourself, just as it was for me as a small escape, or it can be your chains that may lead to other detrimental issues.

So here's an idea. Remember in the introduction I shared with you three stories of families who have experienced something beyond their control called death? Their stories have been re-written. Just as a magician would say "Ta-da!" all is back to normal, let's take a look.

Someone call an ambulance! Get Help! We need help over here! With hundreds of thousands of heartbeats racing to the unknown and unseen finish line. Hundreds of eyes embracing an unwanted, unasked for cinema; multiple minds soaring as far as the cloud would take them, a nightmare is in progress. On just another normal day, 35-year-old Lisa, an account executive at a local agency, has passed out at the office and her life is now at the mercy of her colleagues getting EMS on the scene quick enough.

"Mam, can you hear me?" I have no response team"

"Mam, can you hear me? Help is on the way if you can hear me"

All of a sudden she opens her eyes... she asks, "What happened?"

You fainted, are you ok? he says

Yes, I'm fine. May you get me some water, please?

After that, she was given the privilege to have the rest of the day off. After all, she is the boss.

Hiyaa Dr. I hope you have some good news for me! Exhausted and lethargic, trying to exert what little energy left in his body, Marcus Blain, a 53-year-old man awaits his test results. "There is no easy way to say this to you but the sharp pain that you have been experiencing is only a migraine. Are you just trying to get out of the house again?" In his slyness, Marcus laughs "Listen, when you've been married as long as I have you'd do anything to get out the house!" The room erupts in laughter. "Oh Marcus, are you a piece of work," his wife says. "You do need to take it slow at the gym and give your body time to rest," the Dr says. Marcus Blain is a retired powerlifter that exercises every day and competes in meets. He has no intention of slowing down, but this time he lifted a little too much. His exertion was more than what his body could handle. (He believes he is still in his prime). His wife Maxine, by his side, has the biggest happy grin on her face because she knows her husband is such a jokester and knows how to make her smile. "Dr. Thank you for your time, and I am going to take this one off your hands" Maxine says. As the two prepare themselves to leave they lean into one another for the sweetest kiss. You would have sworn sparks flew.

"Are we there yet? Are we there yet? Are we there yet?" Rose, an overjoyed 7-year-old who is overwhelmed with excitement that it's her first visit to Disneyland, said. She bugged her parents the entire car ride there. Those words will be the only words her parents, Josh and Abigail, will hear as long as they are still driving. Rose will cherish this moment for the rest of her life. Josh and Abigail, although a little annoyed, are just as excited to share this moment with Rose. They love Rose so very much and the look on her face when they finally arrive is what they are looking forward to the most. Although the words "Are we there yet" will haunt them in their dreams for a few days, they will know that it is the result of something special. To them, it's worth it. A little girl was able to see her heroes and experience the wonderful world of magic. Abigail, Josh and Rose finally arrive, and boy oh boy wasn't this worth the wait. Rose can barely contain herself. With her fists clenched, eyes wide open, while looking around she braces herself, bends down, and back up to the most ferocious high pitch scream you have ever heard. Come on mom and dad let's go!!

Voila! How was that? Much better, right? I am so glad that I was able to rewrite their story to have a more desirable ending. How does it make you feel to live in a world of "if only?" Wouldn't it be great to know that we could control death and its fate? Or would that just be too much pressure? It's no secret, I wish my mom was alive, but I'm not too sure that this, rewriting history, would solve the problem. Although yes, the revised version gave me such joy, people will still need help grieving the loss of their loved one. I wish that I could tell you that creating a false imaginary realm would solve this but it won't. There is no single thing that will move you forward in your grief. There just isn't. It will take a series of self-building exercises to achieve healthy grief.

I Can Only, Reality

Earlier, we walked down perfect Patty's perfect neighborhood lane. It was such a pleasant walk and I am sure we'll have another perfect walk again. Not so much. The "reality," is where we live and although I too created an alternative world where my mom was alive where all is well, the reality is where I spend 95% percent of my time. It's real-time feelings and emotions. Real-time observations and real-life situations that are, what they are. There is no change unless the person wants and takes the necessary actions for improvements. I'm sure we've all said at some point in our life "Tell me how you 'really' feel." That statement alone can't be farthest from the truth, as sometimes we just aren't ready to face the truth. Especially when it comes to grief. Don't lie about it, no need to wear a facade. You have to live in your true feelings if you want true relief from your grief. Just as you saw in the previous chapter, I was able to create a seemingly fictitious world that included my mom. The reality is that I was not raised by my mom. I was in the custody of my dad and stepmother and was largely unable to create an "escape" separate from their actions as their reality was a very strong and very present experience for me. Creating an imaginary world for them was impossible as they were (are) alive and grieving in their household was not allowed. They always said "Actions speak louder than words" and boy did they. If you haven't gotten it by now my goal is to see that you began to heal and part of that starts by knowing and sharing your reality. So for your next exercise, do you remember the events that you wrote about early on in this chapter as part of the "I Can Only Imagine" exercise? I want you to take those same events and write down the reality of what happened. Write down how that situation made you feel and why you felt that way. Listen, you have to face the truth. Don't hide from it or sugarcoat either. What's your reality? I'll go first if you like.

"A Real-Life Story"

Mom isn't alive: Surrounded by nothingness, said profoundly by famous American Journalist Hemingway in "A clean well-lighted place," I awake another day. Not sure what today may bring but just know that I am afraid of whatever it is. As a child, I would awake each day to feel unwanted, unloved and hated by the masses starting in the very place that I'm supposed to call home. The discontentment is so thick I can barely breathe. It will suffocate me if I don't get out, and soon. "Hey, it's time to get ready for school. Get up" my dad says. I don't remember too much of anything after that until I arrived at school. I don't remember how my sister and I ended up being separated but we were and I wasn't happy. It was the 1st day of kindergarten. My memory serves me only standing in the hallway waiting for my teacher to come. My dad dropped us off early. As I stand there in the hall crying for you, your back is embedded in my head walking away. That was a tough day for me. Nothing. The wall begins to be built. I know parents have to work, but couldn't this one day be a little less "let's rip the bandaid off" type of day. I'm sure it was for my good, I can only guess. Further down the line, as I came to true understanding and as time went on, things would only get worse with dad and his wife. We (my siblings and I) would be ruled under a new regime with a new dictator, where here and her children will reign as supreme. Anyone dare to come against her or them would be subject to punishment by the punisher, him, our dad as that's pretty much the entirety of his role. Dad checked out a long time ago, probably when our mom, his 1st wife, died, and doesn't have the slightest clue or care how things are being run. He was no longer the "head of household," our new stepmom is/was. Somehow she was able to put a spell on you that had you believing that your children of the deceased 1st wife were being treated with the utmost love and respect. All the while a second family was being created right in the same home where we too lived. Only to be blind to the reality that your children, who are grieving the loss of their mom, were being treated as the ugly red-headed stepchildren that we were to her. Unwanted and in the way of the separate family that was desperately being created without us. Leading up to the day that my twin and I were packing and getting ready to leave for college, a true day of redemption, our stepmother told us in a snarky stern way, "Make sure you take all of your things, don't leave anything behind." Wow, I'm 18 about to embark on an amazing journey, graduated top of my class with scholarships out the wazoo to attend college and those are the parting words. Once our mom died, yes, he married and moved the new family into our house, but the "home" of the surviving 10 children, died right along with our mother and was never intended to be welcomed there. We packed up the vehicle and drove an hour and 30 minutes to our new college. We unloaded the vehicle and put all the boxes in our new dormitory. "All right, that's it, we've got to head back on the road to get back in time." Gave everyone waves of goodbye (No hugs, not that kind of party. What kind of family hugs each other, Ewww) with a smile that wasn't a smile. They left within the time it took to unload the truck and meet the new roommates. That was it. My sister and I had enough love for each other to make it through and that was the happiest and saddest day of my life. We unpacked all of our belongings by ourselves which took so long I believe we were unpacking until about midnight where we had to wake the next morning for class. It was just my twin and I and we had each other's back more than anyone on this planet. I spent the night in awe wondering what's next, lost. Reality set in we had no one but ourselves and each other.

Has the reality set in for you? Has the truth been made clear? The truth is the antidote in which you will be able to get a handle of your grief. That is what you will need to come to terms with, reality. My truth in grief is a little different from yours, as it should be from person to person, due to the realization that I spent most of my life avoiding and suppressing grief as I was in the care of an existent but absent father and his 2nd wife. The reality is that I lived a life feeling completely unsafe wherever I went, home, school, church, the store, as I laid down for sleep, when I woke up, every moment of my life was spent in fear of my life as I had unresolved matters with the abandonment that penetrates from loss. I had no idea that I would make it out. My reality is that I was a child who was not allowed to grieve let alone think about my dead mother. When she died, all memory of her went right in the grave with her. There was absolutely no trace of her existence. All of her belongings were forcibly taken from the home to make way for our "new Mom." One side of the family says one thing and the other side says another but the questionable truth remains; my mother has no place here anymore. "This is the only mom you have," my dad said, referencing his new wife. Later on in life as a teenager, I would find something to change my life with a glimmer of hope. I found a copy of my mother's obituary. My thoughts as a teen were over the hills as I had never seen a picture of her until that time. I was about 17 (again, she died when I was a little over a year). This was gold to me and I cherished it. She exists, I thought. One day, I hung it on my wall near my bed. My thoughts were to welcome my mother back into the home, by posting her picture on the wall alongside where I sleep. One of my older brothers saw it (we shared a room) and said to take it down because dad would not be happy to see that on the wall. That was the extent of the conversation and no other reasoning was shared and by this time in our lives my birth mother was just a figment of my imagination. I was honestly confused, so I took it down and placed it in a keep safe box. One day as I was looking at the obituary in my room, my stepmother came into the room and caught me looking at it. I was like a deer in headlights, stunned and my heart dropped as I didn't know what to expect. Honestly, a little afraid. She then asked to see what I was looking at. She knew exactly what it was and told me to give it to her. She confiscated the obituary from me and said "I will hang on to this in my room. Let me know if you want to look at it." I was mortified, A.) because clearly, I wanted to look at it. That's why I was doing so at that time. B.) What gave her the right to take the only picture that I had of my mom (which I found by mistake might I add). C.) She knew that I would never come to ask her to see the obituary again as they had already created an environment of fear and intimidation in the household that took away our voices beginning as children.

My reality is that I have no clue what it would be like to be raised by the woman who birthed me but I can only hope that it would have been better than what I experienced. My experience lends toward waking up one day, in my youth, to see that the refrigerator had a chain and lock on it. It was placed on there by my stepmother, with dad saying not too much of anything. Later on, the lock came off after about a month. Maybe they realized it was foolish or possibly they grew tired of the process of taking it off and putting it back on multiple times a day. Who knows. My experience is that as a child, the person who I was, my character, my values and morals were controlled by my dad's wife to one day witness her telling him (my dad), in her rage, that he (me) is a habitual liar and a thief in regards to something that I did not do; because I wasn't going to be coerced into taking the bait of being fearful any longer and stood up for myself. Being manipulated, brainwashed and controlled to the max as we, my twin and I, dare not have any "back talk" as that could very well cost us our dinner for the night. My experience is that just as I shared with you before is that there was no safe place for a child needing to grieve, denied a basic right. An entire household of people suffering for years intensely and manifesting toxic behavior due to a significant loss in their lives. Ten children lost their mother, one dad, lost his wife, one stepmother lost her marriage that resulted in divorce, and the child of that union, my step sister, lost her dad and mom when they split; she lost her family. The youngest, skinniest male child in the family, would live a life being threatened, mistreated/bullied and intimidated by my older, much more experienced male siblings and the co-parents in the household; and as a grieving child would experience the same treatment in grade school.

So how does a child have a childhood? The answer to that, is that he doesn't, he survives and wonders each day, "will he make it to the next." On top of losing mom, ten children lost their childhood. Although this book is dedicated to those that have experienced loss due to death, loss in any form takes on the same principles as grief, i.e. loss due to a divorce. The focus here is on death as it traditionally accompanies a wide variety of other losses that are sometimes challenged by those around you. Loss of relationships, loss of status, loss of health, loss of friendships/relationships, loss of security, etc. One of the main questions children have after losing a parent is, "Who will care for me?" "Who's going to look after me?" These questions can go unanswered and sometimes manifests in other attachments. Let me explain to you what I mean. One day after my family had just left church. I was maybe nine or 10 and the entire family was outside talking.

This was special for me because my oldest brother, who was about 22 years of age, his wife and children had come to visit us as well. I was innately happy to see them because I hadn't seen them in a while. So we all finished talking and my brother and his family were going to come back to our parent's house with the rest of the family. I wanted to ride with him, as I typically rode with him before. I ran to his car, opened the door and there wasn't much space for me. His two children, my nephews, were in their car seats along with another of my young siblings sitting in the middle. His wife sat in the front seat. In my saddening disappointment that there was no space for me, I said in a jokingly but happy way, "Awe man, all the Rugrats have taken up all the space" smiled and left the car. Remember my brother wasn't in the car yet. I guess his wife didn't like that I called them "Rugrats" because about five to seven minutes later my brother approached me and said, "Hey, let me talk to you real quick." So I paused and waited for him to talk to me. At some point, he ended up physically hurting me and no one knew. I had to hide it as I was afraid of what would happen. (I won't go into too much detail on the injury and the confrontation because my love for him is out of this world. It was a confusing time for us all. My goal is to illustrate the many situations one, especially a child, may encounter after the death of a very important person that pen points significant moments in life where relationships, security and safety, began to tarnish resulting in more isolation.) My brother left saying, "Don't you ever in your life call my kids Rugrats again or you and I will have a problem." I was shocked and confused because in my mind, a nine-year-old kid, "Rugrats" are the endearing cute little smart kids from the cartoon called "Rugrats." It was only the hottest cartoon every kid was watching and I was proud to see them in his backseat. I too wanted to be a Rugrat. Side note, If you don't know the cartoon Rugrats, look it up immediately. I promise you will fall in love with them. Tommy Pickles, the twins Phil and Lil, Chucky, Suzie, Angelica, they are to die for. I loved that show and loved his kids, but I can only assume that the translation from his wife to him wasn't the greatest. My brother too, was in a transitional place as his marriage was not welcomed by our guardians. So anything that sparked from that incident was in direct correlation. That moment, along with many moments prior and after affected my grieving greatly, challenged everything in my life, and left me wondering, who will protect me? Because to me, I lost my whole family. Because he was the oldest when our mom died, there was a small amount of attachment that I had toward him, as any younger brother would have for his older sibling, as he was the closest thing to sharing her legacy with the younger children but it was halted by a long line of discrepancies. The reality is that people will endure moments of hardship when their loved one dies, where grieving is just a word and not a process; and "pray for the bereaved" was just another sentence to say during the funeral service. Would it have been different if they were alive? Different? Yes. Better? We just don't know.

Grieving can come at any point in our lives. As illustrated above, it's not just one incident that can contribute to an unhealthy environment that's not viable for grief, it's a culmination of events and incidents. Your events will be completely different than mine. This is why you must take immediate action as soon as possible whether you lost your loved one as an adult or you are assisting your children with their grief. Grieving is a process that takes time and with the right people around you, it will set you up for success. You have to open your heart and accept healing. Just as you will experience different emotions and events during your grief some of them you'll have control over and some things you won't. Some days you will experience extreme sadness while other days you will have blissful joy, but you must be willing to live one more day and fight for your relief. Losing a loved one is hard. But it doesn't have to be if you are willing to be vulnerable with yourself and those around you. Open your heart and mind. When you feel something don't be afraid to express it. We are taught from a very early age, especially men, to "suck it up." Think back to when you had your 1st splinter and you even attempted to cry. Those words are likely your dad's 1st reaction if not your older brother trying to "toughen you a little" when trying to remove it. I implore you to be as vulnerable as you want and I am certain you will feel a load lift off your shoulder.

Mothers Day has always been a difficult holiday for me to celebrate. It was difficult in my grade school years because my sibling and I were forced to celebrate our stepmother as being the only mother and overtime it became pointless and lacked true emotion surrounding the holiday. The sincerity and gratefulness became dull responses that lacked genuineness. If I was going to be forced to honor one and banish the other, I wanted nothing to do with it. Therefore, I stopped celebrating it once I moved out, at age 18, for college. My biological mother never surfaced for us during the holidays. She was always left out and never remembered or thought of let alone spoken of. Later on, about three years after college I began to truly grieve, and it became an even harder day for me. One, because I felt that I was robbed all those years of truly honoring my mother and two, because I truly wanted to know of her as I missed her dearly. Each year it hits me, my mom's memory has been shattered and disintegrated and I blamed my dad and stepmom for this for a long time. Not of her death, but the memory of her. Mothers Day, May 7, 2016, at 11:02 pm. I could barely sleep. I was alone in my one-bedroom apartment and all the emotions and past came rushing back to me all at once like a waterfall. It was too overwhelming for me so I wrote a letter to her that changed my life thereafter and I want to share it with you.

Until the Night Takes Me - Morgan Hale

Until the night takes me,
I'll be here by your side.
Loving you until the very day I see your face
Then love you even more.
Never knew you,
And if you showed today
Your face would be just
A blur.
Would I recognize you when I see you?
Will you recognize me when you see me?
I question.
I've changed since you last saw me.
I've grown since you last held me.
I don't think you would,
It's impossible,
It's been far too long.
No Way!
I barely recognize myself

But they say a mother recognizes her child?
Maybe just one day or two, or three, or four or five...
Maybe, just come back to me,
and all will be well.
Why?
Just. Why?

The proverbial scars that protrude on our hearts once a loved one dies, has catastrophic pain when ripped. The panic and terror that derives from such turn of events can leave the strongest beast immobile. This is life-changing and what you are experiencing is real. From adults and children alike understanding that it will take you owning your truth is a sure path into healthy mourning and grief.

A CHILD'S SILENT
PLEA FOR HELP

D eath is not a joke and it definitely shouldn't be taken lightly. As a part of all obituaries, there is a section called "the survivors" where it lists everyone that a person has left behind. It lists the aunts, uncles, cousins, the widow or the widower and the children, if there were any. Now, when it comes to grieving, for most it can be a very selfish process. Especially, as adults. Let's think of (and when I "think," know that I am referring to real-life situations and experiences) a nice family: two adults, three children, ages nine, six, and three. They are living a life of love and happiness where one day dad doesn't come home. He falls asleep at the wheel after a long day of work and ends up in a car accident that claimed his life. Police arrive at the wife's home to tell her the news and it breaks her heart. She eventually brings herself together enough to have the "dad isn't coming home" talk with her three children. The wife is left distraught and helpless. A significant number of adults in the family come to the aid of her in her time of need and look to do as much as they can to help her back to herself. She rejects help from some, as her trust levels have gone done and feel completely alone in the situation. She is left with three children to raise on her own. The children are comforted by grandma. After about six months to a year, things seem to be normal. The support from family isn't as prevalent as it used to be as of course they have their own lives to lead (and of course she should be done grieving, right? Wrong). Mom seems to be managing her emotions just enough to make it through another day. What about the children?

This may come as a shock to some of you but if you haven't figured it out by now, children grieve too. We see adults flock to other adults to comfort each other at funerals and so forth. Which is excellent, keep doing that. We tell the surviving parent "I am sorry for your loss" and is likely going to hear that many times within a single hour. Flowers are sent to the families home and maybe even gifts but what does all this mean to the child that has also been affected? When does the child receive this same level of support? Children are comforted during this time but not to the extent

to which the adult will be comforted. I mean, let's face it, the capability to understand and grasp what happening isn't quite there for some children but I guarantee you that they know that something has shifted in their lives. Their grief will be displayed in other reactions. What you do next as the surviving parent will determine the hope and future of your children. It sounds like a lot of pressure and it is. It's the territory that comes with being a parent. I'm certain that you would have never thought that you would be raising children on your own but we have to capture the power in this situation. Your responsibility is to not only grieve the death of your spouse but to also see that your children have a healthy grieving process. Get this, you don't have to do it alone either. That is what this chapter is all about. It's about the children that often get lost in the whirlwind of the surviving spouses' grief unable to express themselves. It's about children having the right to grieve as well because just like the slogan says, "Kids are people too" and here's another one, "No Child left behind." Those are popular phrases that give the recognition that is long overdue to the mental state and wellbeing of our children.

When I was about 14 or 15, one of my older brothers got married to his long time girlfriend. I believe he was about 25 or 26 years of age. It was a beautiful ceremony. We laughed, we ate and from my perspective, it was a pretty good day.

At the wedding reception, they showed a slideshow of their journey. I did not pay too much attention to it at the time. I was a teenager just along for the ride. (Of course, I was happy for my brother, I just kind of grew up with little to no emotion). In the slideshow, there were pictures of them and pictures of the family. Everyone seemed to enjoy the presentation. My brother and his wife wanted to share the slideshow with everyone that attended. So as a part of the thank you gifts, everyone went home with a DVD copy of the slideshow, so that they too can cherish it forever. (To this day I'm not sure if the DVD exists by the way). Later on, in the month My dad and step-mother decided to relive the moment and wanted to watch the DVD, so they did. As kids, we all gathered in their bedroom to watch it on their TV. This was now my opportunity to see what all the excitement was over the slideshow. The slideshow was put together pretty well and had wonderful music. However, that's not the reason why I left the room and cried myself to sleep that night. As the slideshow went on we saw archived pictures of his wife's family and my family. Cousins, uncles, the dates that they went on, etc. I'm talking old pictures too, it was all there. Some of the people in the pictures I knew and some I didn't as it was pictures from before I was even thought of in most cases. Then, all of a sudden a picture of a young woman and five kids came on the screen as a part of the slideshow presentation. She was standing holding an infant child and the others were standing in front of and around her. Seeing that she looked familiar to me and my certainty of who the lady was in the picture, but wasn't too sure at the same time, I said out loud to my dad and step-mother "Who is that? Is that Aunt Mave? (Aunt Mave was married to my dad's brother). My dad quickly, in his frustration with a loud angry voice, screamed at me saying "NO BOY! THAT'S YOUR MOTHER! DO YOU NOT KNOW WHO YOUR OWN MOTHER IS?" I looked back at him, with wide eyes in complete silence afraid, confused and stunned by his reaction. I saw his face brows and forehead clenched like the grinch and eyes bloodshot red. I can tell he was pissed that asked that question. Remember in the preface I told you that every trace of my mom's existence had been wiped from our home? Yes, that included pictures as well. I had absolutely no idea who the woman in the picture was and made a genuine guess.

At that moment I felt humiliated. I felt alone and most of all I felt so stupid. I sat in that stew of emotions awaiting for the slide show to end. I was no longer interested. He was right. How can I not know who my mom was? So yeah, I went on that night and wept silently. I shared a room with my brother and didn't want him to know that I was having a breakdown. I was ashamed. There was no follow-up conversation to check on me, or even just to question why I thought that would be an aunt and not mom. But let us rewind a little. My dad was angry with me for asking that question as to place the blame on me, and yes I blamed myself. However, that's simply not the case. I was not at fault. As you learned in the previous text, in all of the 14/15 years of my life following her death, my mother was never spoken of from either my dad and definitely not my stepmother. Not from siblings either. I was never privy to seeing a picture of her, especially since I hadn't found her obituary at this point in my life yet and we were completely estranged from my mother's side of the family. The severity of it is if I was walking down the street as a child and if a stranger walked up to me and said he was my uncle, aunt, or even mom for that reason, I would be conflicted. How can I, as a child, know who my mother is let alone how she looks if this information wasn't shared with me? That's confusing. Am I to automatically know who she is? Somehow in this situation, I was expected to just know. All I knew was that a woman that gave birth to ten children, including me, died and that she was replaced by a new woman slated to be our "said mom."

Could you imagine being a 14/15-year-old not knowing who your parents are? When you have one surviving parent and they have not yet gathered the slightest strength or freedom to have a conversation about mom with their children, I must say it. It's outright selfish. The sad part is that many children have come to know what this feeling is. Yes, my dad lost his wife, but it doesn't stop there. 10 children also lost their mom with the youngest being a little over 12 months. "I too grieve, dad." Silently spoken by every child without their mom. "I too grieve, mom," said by every child that is missing their deceased father. It's not enough for you as parents to manage your grief and forget about the children that you chose to bring into this world. It's just not enough for you as parents to suppress your grief to only never speak of your deceased spouse ever again while your children watch you from the bedroom suffer day after day. It's just not enough. Sure, this is hard to hear, but I assure you that It's the truth. Your children need you and you need your children. I will say it one last time! If you are the guardians of the surviving children you have a responsibility to the kids that you agreed to welcome into your home and raise on behalf of their parents. You were either chosen by either the parents leaving them to you in their will or by making you godparents. Maybe you didn't ask for it. However, for some reason, they trusted that you would be the best fit for their child in the event something was to happen to them. Maybe you won a custody trial? It doesn't matter the circumstance. You should get out of your way and do your best to help your children succeed by helping them manage their grief. If you find that you are unable to, it's time to outsource assistance from professionals.

Children are hard to figure out but they shouldn't be because guess what? We've all been children before. It's no secret. What happens is that as we get older, life starts to throw boulders at us and we forget what it's like to be a kid. Subsequently forgetting how they once felt as a child and the true support that they needed to succeed. I am certain that some, if not most of you, have stated as an adolescent, "I'm not going to do this when I have children" (in some nature of that syntax). Thus dubbing yourself as a future better parent having no interest in doing things the way your parents did. After all your purpose in stating that was to make certain that your future children had the emotional and physical support that you felt was at a shortage for you. You without a doubt wanted your children to have a better life. Now that you have them, they still can, even with one parent or guardian.

A child's response to their parent's death (or death in general) will be different from those of an adult. Do not expect them to react the same way that you do for you to notice that they are grieving. It can be hard to spot if you do not know what the indicators are. It can also be hard to recognize if you, as the surviving adult, are consumed in your grief to notice. I want you to be on your toes at the first sign of change in your children. This is where you as a parent should shine as you should know if there is a change in your child's behavior after all your behavior has changed as well. You just lost your spouse. Now, the immediate following weeks and even months after the death are crucial for both you and your children but know that if you have young children their understanding grief may not come until later when they are a little older and can span throughout adulthood. Children at different ages experience grief at different cycles in their life.

The American Academy of Child & Adolescent Psychiatry released an article in 2018 detailing signs of grieving children. A few things that you should be on the lookout for:

A. Excessively imitating the dead person

B. Withdrawal from friends

C. A sharp drop in school performance

D. Believing that they are talking to or seeing the deceased family member for an extended period of time.

E. Repeated statements of wanting to join the dead person

F. An extended period of depression, in which the child loses interest in daily activities and events.

G. Inability to sleep, loss of appetite.

H. Prolonged fear of being alone.

Now, of course, these are not the only signs that you should be aware of and this does not mean that your child will exhibit all of these in their grief. Every child is different. They are trying to figure this out and make sense of it all just as you are. You should make every attempt to be there for your children. You also may say, "What if my child doesn't have any of the signs and seems to be doing pretty well with everything? He or she has been pretty quiet about it and haven't asked any questions." Then it's time for you to ask them questions. Assuming is not the way to go when it comes to your grieving children. Just think if all the adults around you saw you "being strong" as you seem to be taking everything pretty well and they decide to leave you to your grief. They assumed that you were ok but on the inside, you were crying out for some kind of help and direction. Maybe you're too proud to ask for help or even just a warm hug. Perhaps you're just like me and have a high emotional capacity and tend to show no emotion at all. You begin to harbor feelings to make decisions, so you sit in silence thinking long and hard. If that's the case, what about your children. Typically the apple doesn't fall too far from the tree. They could be just as proud, or a true processor at heart where their thoughts and emotions live together resulting in them talking themselves down for a little while. If that's not the case, just know that they have no clue where to begin to even know grief and what it means to them. Even the hardest of people will still melt in a hug, especially, by the right person, and as a parent, you are exactly the right person

As the surviving parent (and when I say "parent" in this way, know that I am talking about legal guardians as well) you have a major role to play in the child's path through grief. I am sure you are wondering now that you know some of the signs to look for, what next? I'm glad you asked. In retrospect to it all, what you should be doing is allowing your child freedom and openness with you to grieve. This will need to be done with progressive and conducive management. You can simply do this by having a conversation with your child about their dead parent. Tell them stories that they may have never heard before like, how the two of you met, their favorite things to do and even speak about a time in which the dead parent did a specific activity with the child. Make sure that the child knows that their deceased loved one is connected to them with memories that they can hold on to and cherish. When I was about 17 or 18 years old, we had pulled into the driveway to our house. I believe we were coming home from school. My dad had picked up all the kids like he typically did (I appreciated that he was the one to drop us off for school and pick us up. This meant a lot in the long run). As we pulled in everyone got out of the car. I was sitting in the front seat. For some reason that I don't quite remember why my dad asked to stay behind in the car. It seemed odd. Typically, when he wanted to talk to me alone it would only mean one thing. That I was in trouble for something and that my teacher possibly called him while he was at work to share how bad of a student I was that day (although yes, I would sometimes get scolded in front of all the family, you never knew some days). As my heart pounded faster and faster, sitting on the edge of my seat, I grew more anxious as everyone got out of the car. I did not know what he needed to share with me and I needed to be quick to provide some sort of excuse to get out of trouble. The ride home was quiet, as usual. Then, low and behold the conversation was about my mother (his deceased wife). He then shared with me a story surrounding her death and gave me little insight into her personality. It was an interesting conversation that lasted about 5 minutes. He ended the conversation by saying that if I ever had questions about her that I should go to him and that he would tell me what I wanted to know. As I sat silently, I didn't know what to say or what to ask him. After all, I was in my senior year of high school, I was in the process of preparing for college with an unhealthy relationship with him. At that point, for me, it was too late as I no longer cared to have that conversation, especially with him. I had begun counting down the days until I graduated high school. This wasn't out of disrespect for him or my mom, but at this point in my life, I had just begun to shape who I was without them. I had a lot happening in my world (doesn't all 17-year-olds). Although this conversation came by surprise, I can say that at that time, I can't begin to tell you how much I appreciated that moment of openness and vulnerability by him.

I share that to say, parents, do not wait. The time is now. Yes, even while you are grieving you must help your child to grieve as well. Some children may grieve later on in life because they didn't know the parent as well. I know, I did. I didn't begin to feel free to grieve my mother's death until my last few months of college when I was approaching my graduation ceremony. You're grieving but do you as a parent allow your child to grieve? I ask that you allow your children to grieve. It's ok. Please do not take that away from them. They deserve to know all that you know about your deceased partner. Don't ignore the signs or dismiss the behaviors to be growing pains, or that the child is maturing or worse, nothing. I never said that this would be easy as this will be difficult for a lot of parents. Especially if the surrounding factors of your loved one's death isn't the greatest. Was it murder? How about your spouse being in a coma and becoming brain dead? Maybe there was suicide involved, or how about attempted murder? Perhaps the last words you said weren't the kindest. Whew! That has to be tough and I applaud you for being consistent to continue living and pursuing.

Another thing that you can do to see that you help your child grieve, is to celebrate. Remember I stated that your role is to make sure that your child feels safe and open in expressing their feelings. So now it's time to celebrate and what are you celebrating you ask? How about your loved ones' birthday, Christmas, Thanksgiving, Valentine's Day, the child's birthday, celebrate them just for being a kid and even national chocolate chip cookie day. Your celebrations could be limitless. Now I'm not saying that you need to break the bank celebrating every holiday that pops up in the world (there are national days for everything). What I am saying is that you will need to create an atmosphere that condones love and growth in grief. Statements that I want you to think about is; I never want my child to wonder if they are loved by their deceased parent; I never want them to wonder if they are proud of them. Celebrating will create a sense of belonging. When you celebrate, don't forget to invite the most important people, ie the deceased side of the family. This too is as equally important as creating an environment of openness and truth. Your child needs to experience them. For some, this may be a challenge. As the surviving parent, you will have to place a few boundaries on what it means for relatives to interact with your children. If it is a toxic environment, that will be even tougher but you must remain calm and figure out what's best for the child and proceed from there. Reassure them, validate their emotions and help them through it. Without it, your children will spend their time in an identity crisis. Think about it. A child is a product of two people. When one parent dies, when the child is young, It only leaves one parent left. That child will grow up to know the surviving parent and understand where they get certain traits from. They will grow up only knowing half of the story. They'll feel like there is a missing piece. If you haven't done this properly, then rest assured that your child feels that something is missing. The truth is that they are correct in their feelings. Something is missing, and it's their parent. You have the golden opportunity to sow wonderful memories into your child about their deceased parent. If you want them to have the full scope of their parents, maybe schedule a playdate with their grandmother (the mom of the deceased), or the aunts and uncles (brothers and sisters). Of course, you will need to tell them the truth but you owe them that. This will make your child feel whole again.

In some cases, when a partner of a young parent dies, the surviving parent of young children may either vow to never get in a relationship or marry ever again. Some choose to get remarried either soon or when the children get older.

Whatever the choice, honor it and live life prosperously. For this next chapter, I want to discuss the implication of those that decide to remarry early, with young children, rather than later because they will too play a vital role in the development of your child that has lost their parent to death. There are a few things added to the equation that you need to be aware of in understanding the dynamics of a blended family. Things to think about. Do you want more children? If so, that means you will indefinitely have children that are half-siblings. So how do you handle this? Maybe your new spouse has children as well and you will be welcoming not only a new step-parent into your child's life but a new step-sibling(s) as well. Things just got complicated, right? I know! Don't worry I will spell it out for you. It can be the biggest, happiest family that ever walks the earth if you employ all the right tools needed by welcoming new people into your child's life. Welcoming your new spouse into the home and your new children, whether step or half, all the while not neglecting the child that will grieve for an indefinite time frame, is crucial.

When a step-parent gets involved (even before marriage), it's time for a serious conversation about the role he or she will play in your child's life. Let me remind you that this section of the book is all about the child and what's best for them and their grief. Sometimes we forget this during our personal walk, so I want to bring you back to the goal here, to see that your child can grieve. In this conversation, you, as the surviving parent, need to be clear on a few things in regards to your new partner. The first thing is that there needs to be a clear understanding that your previous partner is dead and that, dead, doesn't mean forgotten. After all, you didn't choose to end the marriage in a divorce of that person. This was forced upon you where you had no choice. You will need to focus your new-found love on your new relationship, with the understanding that reversion of habits and talks of this person will happen. Not only will talks of your dead loved one happen, but you might also display an emotional reaction to that person. Be sure to assure your new partner that it's harmless and is not a reflection of the current relationship status. That kind of behavior and expectation should not be too much different in how you communicate when talking about an ex from a previous, but relationship with a slight difference. This person is completely different from your deceased husband or wife, so don't try to force them to be like that person. The second thing is you will need to decide on how your child will address your new partner. Will your child call this new parent, "dad/mom." Will they call them by their first name, or how about Mr. or Mrs. Lauder (by the last name) or is there a nickname? You may not think that this is important but forcing a child to call their "new parent" mom or dad can have opposite effects of what you are trying to accomplish. You never want your child to believe that their biological parent is being wiped from their memory and being replaced. This can interrupt the grieving process. The third thing is preserving memories for your child. Should you remove images and items that belong to your deceased spouse? This is a double edge sword because the answer is yes and no. Yes, you should remove a good amount of things so of course, a new partner can feel comfortable and at ease. On the flip side, you mustn't remove everything as remember your child needs this to continue grieving and be freed from it. Keep a few pictures on the mantle, and even give your child a few pictures or keepsakes as well. Remember your child is going to have to adjust to a new adult in their world while grieving the death of their parent. You will need to have multiple conversations with your child surrounding the things that you'll keep in the household to uncover boundaries of respect. The fourth thing that your new partner understands is that there will be conversations about the dead partner with your child and their role is to support this on both ends. Your child needs to know that the new blended family does not exclude the biological parent that has passed. Your new partner will need to be on board with this to see that your child does not feel alone in their time of grief. The sooner you can capture the essence of a blended family the better. The fifth thing I want you to have a discussion around is step-children (if any) and half children (of course you will need to decide if you want more children from the start). Like I said toward the beginning, you are about to welcome a new adult and possibly a new child that wasn't there before into your child's life. Things will be different. You'll need to discuss how you plan to discipline, interact and overall integrate the children. Depending on the ages, you can't just put them together and expect magic. The children, as well as the new partner, will need to be well integrated before marriage while maintaining these conversations. Why is this important you ask? "That's my mom" or "That's my dad" little Johnny says to his new brother Adam. As a parent, I am certain that you will love this new child as you own. At least that's my hope. You will show unconditional love and support to a new child. This could be threatening to your child as he or she could feel possessive yet excluded. All children will need to be treated equally. This will be a challenge as you innately don't think that there is a difference. Understand that there is a difference and moving forward implementing these steps will improve the quality of your blended family tremendously. Children are impressionable and a child that has lost their parent will need the support on a long term basis.

A child grieving the death of a parent alone will have complications. Just as you grieve your child will grieve as well. It will be different than you. Don't expect the waterworks, the screaming, the yelling, etc. True, some of these things can and will happen during your child's grief but don't assume that if these signs are absent then your child is doing well with the death. There are no perfect signs. If you are feeling helpless and that you have reached a point where you can't assist, I urge you to reach out to professionals as quickly as possible. There are plenty of resources and great therapists out there that will see that your child has the help he or she needs. These observations and steps are meant to be a stepping stone to taking control of your grief. Your role is to be as open as possible to ensure your child feels safe. Reassure your child that you are in their corner and things will get better; because they will. Invite your child to have those conversations with you and when they get comfortable enough they will start coming to you. When they do come to you, honor that time. Do not dismiss it because it caught you off guard or it's not the best time to talk about it. Explore it. It was brought up at that time for a reason and ignoring it will put a strain on their progress. I'm sure you want the best for your child. See that you show up for your child in an amazing way.

GRIEVING THE LIFE AND DEATH OF A LOVED ONE

Everything we went over in the chapters above will help you sustain reading the remainder of this book now that you have an understanding of the foundation. My theory is that everything will fall into place naturally. You won't have to work as hard because you will always have a firm foundation. Grieving the life and death of a loved one has its challenges and is perplexing in a lot of different ways. It's also very unique to each one of you. Now let's continue in the process.

According to US Funerals, the average funeral can cost anywhere between $8,000 - $10,000. Wow. Here is a list of what you'll have to plan for when your loved one dies, and if you are reading this book as you have lost someone here is what you have already been through. The cost of a headstone, cost of a casket, cost of the gravesite, embalming, cost of a grave liner, cost to dig the grave, vendor fees if you want to use the funeral home and funeral directors services fee. On top of all the stress that you have/are going through, you now have the responsibility to lay your loved one to rest, then you may begin your resting phase as well. Let's be honest, that's a lot to handle and my head hurts just thinking about this process. Although, yes, one should plan a funeral after finding out their loved one has passed, just as you plan a wedding once a couple is engaged, however, we are dealing with a completely different set of emotions guiding our everyday thoughts and actions.

After you've gone through the planning process it is time for the funeral, time for you to say goodbye one last time. At this moment, I want you to think about the funeral of your loved one. Yes, I want you to kind of relive that moment just for a while. If you have not yet gone to the funeral, I want you to think about the perfect "see you later" moment with your loved one. Also, for those of you that couldn't bear to see your loved one in that way and decided not to go to the funeral for your reasons, or maybe you stayed outside in the parking lot, I want you to think of this moment as well.

For those of you that have experienced the funeral already, think about yourself and how you felt at that moment. Think of the smell, the weather for the day, the flowers and the music. I also want you to think about who was sitting next to you. Did someone hold your hand or hug you? Maybe some comforting words were exchanged. Did you cry, or maybe you were forced to keep it together for the family as you are the strong one that they look to for their strength? Did you have to console an irate aunt or an uncle? Was there animosity present at the funeral? Were there uninvited guests? This may be overwhelming for you to recapture these moments and if it does take a moment and breathe. I remember when I was about 15 years old, one of my uncles died. I first began to know my uncle Mark at a very young age, possibly eight or nine. All I knew was that he was a very large man both in height and weight. He was morbidly obese and had quite a few health issues. He was my dad's youngest brother. He became an uncle that I looked at in admiration because he was so good at playing the piano. He could play anything without looking at the keys and read music well. I was impressed, to say the least. One day, we went to a burger place and he ordered me a children's meal. We then went to the grocery store where he bought me my very own bag of grapes. I remember this because although I rarely saw him, I cherished this moment as a child. Fast forward some years later to his funeral. Let me remind you that I did not see him often so growing up he kind of became a blur but what I did remember was that he was a large man that could barely walk. On the day of his funeral, as now I am a teenager, I viewed the body one last time. When I saw him, unfortunately, I didn't recognize him as the uncle that I remembered. This was in part due to the amount of work that they had to do to him to have him fit in a casket and also due to the effects of his health issues. When our loved ones die, no matter what the circumstance is, we are wired to love the person that we once knew. I ask you one final question of reflection. Was the person in the casket the person you remember them to be?

Maybe you haven't gone to the funeral yet. Have you thought about how you would say goodbye? I am certain you have conjured up at least a thousand different scenarios on how you would say it. Have you thought about the way you would compose yourself at the funeral? Are you starting to reminisce on a previous funeral you attended where maybe you weren't your best self? Are you dreading the moment as you are unsure what to expect? Maybe you're estranged from the family and don't feel that you belong or that you don't deserve to feel what you are feeling. Maybe you're feeling guilty. You're likely still confused, wondering what's next. Death brings about so many different scenarios of behavior from those surviving. Although it may seem that I have covered all the bases, I am sure that I have only scratched the surface when it comes to the amount of stress and pressure that one has and will go through to grieve the loss of their loved one. I asked you to recall that day for a reason. All of this is important to understand what you as an individual are facing when it pertains to your mental health surrounding the loss. All of those factors played a major role in how you decided to cope with your grief. So when you are 10 times as hard on yourself or someone says "I know he died two years ago, but you have to get over this," know that you have dealt with a lot and you have the right to take your time in understanding how you feel while moving forward. While you are being judged for dealing with grief after two years, did you know that even in relationships that tend to be happy, will go through a honeymoon phase? Get this, Couples Therapy Inc published a research article in 2018 that stated that this honeymoon phase can last up to 30 months and some may be shorter of course. Now, I'm not saying that this is a good thing. As I am sure some will say that there are risks in the honeymoon phase, but let's face it, they are living in a blissful world where their partners are perfect in every way. The love is apparent, acceptance is apparent and every little nuance is adorable. After a while, the honeymoon phase wears off, as it will inevitably. Once it wears off, some will have a hard time adjusting and maybe don't make it, but for others they do and here's why. The article goes on to share how couples "survive" the end of the honeymoon phase. The couples have to take intentional steps to build trust and commitments to each other. This can be done by doing things that they have never done before and even exploring in the bedroom; however if all else fails, the article suggests couples therapy. So listen, don't think that you are the only one that will have to experience a phase of recovery from something and please don't feel bad for feeling for someone you have lost. This is natural, so accept it and move forward.

When you first found out your loved one passed, I'm sure it broke your heart. Then you had to deal with laying that person to rest within the week and I'm sure that process wasn't fun at all. Now you are stuck with your thoughts and feeling lost. Here is what I need you to do and if it hasn't registered with you yet, I need you to grieve. Here's how. During my time as a grief coach, I developed a curriculum that walks participants through a few steps to assist a person in their grief. For this chapter, you will need your workbook. Let us focus on three action steps that I think would be substantial in moving you forward in your grief. Let's start with the first one.

Get It off your chest

Action step number one is all about getting things out of you. If you are more of an introverted person, like me, this should be easy for you as I am sure you have had a lot of time with your thoughts (inserts laughing emoji). But seriously, this won't be an easy task for you introverts because we naturally bottle all of our feelings inwardly until one day we explode or "forget about it" (in other words suppressed feeling). That's unfair to yourself. You have to give yourself a fighting chance at a healthy way of grieving. Extroverts, you're not off the hook here either as you are just as confused if not angry during this time as well. What is holding on to it on going to do but destroy the humanity left in you? Here's what I want you to do. I want you to be very attentive to yourself. When you are ready to do the exercise, I want you to close your eyes. I want you to imagine the day you found out that your loved one was dead. Think of the entire day from the time you woke up until the time in which you finally went to sleep. Think of your emotions. What did you have for breakfast that day? What was the last thing you said to that person? Stay in that moment for about 2-5 minutes. When you're ready open your eyes and write. Leave nothing omitted. If you need to take a moment to breathe or get some fresh air, I urge you to take it but I suggest that you not parlay the healing process. I told you from the beginning that I will be with you along this journey. Allow me to share. Please note that my sharing of the day will be a little different, as all stories should, due to the timing. I call this exercise "Time to explode."

"Time to explode"

Where do I begin, is the question? I was so young when you died. I don't remember you, let alone the day that you died. I was only 18 months. I'm not too sure how but some reason as I got a little older I knew you were nowhere to be found, and I knew that the woman that my dad remarried wasn't you, my mother. How can that be when you were never spoken of. What I do hope is that you died with love in your heart for your children. The older I get I question if you died feeling lonely. The stories that are shared about you just don't add up to who I believe you to be. There are missing pieces to the puzzle. It has to be. If I had to zone in on the moment in which I knew you weren't coming back or dead one might say, it must have been when I was about three or four years old. Dad called all the children into his bedroom as he and his wife had something they wanted to say. At this time in my life, he was married to his new wife, of whom as a child I automatically called "mom" because I was so young to distinguish. He began to talk and I don't remember much, but they told all of us that from now on, that all the children would call her mom. For me, I was a bit confused because I, (as a toddler) was already calling her mom although I knew innately that she wasn't. My older siblings were shocked by this request because they initially were calling her by her first name, Lisa. They were extremely unhappy about this mandate. This would be part of the transition of removing our mom from our lives. The atmosphere wasn't pleasant. As a confused toddler, I began to question the situation where I wondered "Why are they forcing us to call his new wife, mom, if she is not our mom?" I was conflicted in wanting the best for my siblings but still didn't quite understand what was happening. If there was ever a moment, this was it.

You may either take this time to complete the exercise as a follow along, you may choose to complete the exercise after reading it, or you may choose to complete the exercise as you read for the second time. Whatever works for you, know that I support it. You may also choose to "get it off your chest" by sharing it with a professional or a friend. That will work too. Take your time and be in the moment. This might sting but you will get through it, even if your teardrops fall on the paper. I promise it will dry. When you are finished I want you to read it out loud to yourself or maybe just read it in your head, but please read it again. When you do, if you forgot something, add that in there too. Remember your goal is to get everything off your chest. You have to let go of it all.

Congratulations you've just made the first step in learning to let go. Haven't you heard the age-old proverb of, "You'll do more damage by holding on, than letting go?" At least I believe that's how it goes, in so many words. The purpose of letting go doesn't mean that you should cause yourself to forget your loved one. Make no mistake that this is an exercise to get you to release all the pain, all the hurt and all the sorrow out of your heart. It is causing you to lose sight of who you are. When we think of our loved ones, it places us in a place of happiness. We tend to go down the memory lane where everything was perfect because he or she was alive. After a while, this seems normal and proactive in assisting you in your grief. This can have one of two effects. You can take those memories and thoughts to lead you down a healthy remembrance of your loved one. In which you do this by pausing to recognize that the thoughts of your loved one were fun and brought joy to your life; then proceed to accept the things you cannot change. Thus allowing yourself to be open to your loved one showing up in various ways of your life. That's something to look forward to right? It's kind of mysterious. The second option is that you may get in your thoughts and go down memory lane to get lost in them. Once you're lost you have to try and find your way back. By that time, you've begun to deeply miss this person and want them back at that very instant. You begin to believe that you're alone in your feelings. Everything becomes wrong, with nothing being right, now that they are not here. Why would this person leave you like this, don't they know that you are not strong without them? Have you found yourself digging that hole? I know I have, and it doesn't feel good at all. I want you to know that you are in the right place, you do love, everything is becoming right because you are working on it, and you are not alone my friend.

Family time means that I'm all alone

As we move right along to our next action step, we'll learn the different dynamics of how to harness your feelings of being alone. For some odd reason, when we lose someone near and dear to us, death has a way of making everyone impacted feel like they are alone (if you allow it). I have uncovered the "not so" hidden secret to this. Are you ready? Here's the reason why. It's because we do not talk about it. When there is death in our circle, where the feeling of loneliness and death has taken power over them, it blocks our ability to be expressive. We curl into our pity as to say, "no one else gets it." We wrap ourselves in our tears with the intent to drown ourselves in the Atlantic ocean as surely no one will find you lost at sea. We guard ourselves in a fort protecting it with cannonballs and firearms from any intruder that's approaching as surely it must be a monster of some sort. After all, you are the only one left of your kind believing your entire village of people has been destroyed. When this happens our grief from death has won and truly our victory is in choosing to live.

This next exercise will be a stretch and partly easy. This will be a challenge for some of you. Action step number 2 is about getting those you call family involved. I want you to write down every person's name, or their nickname to make it personal, in your immediate family or circle that has grieved the loss of your loved one. For example, if in a family of 6 that includes Mom, Dad, four teenage children, that lost grandma on mom's side of the family. The true immediate circle would be a mom and her siblings plus the grandpa. (I hope that wasn't confusing). After that, I then want you to create a list of a secondary list of family members and friends whose grandma loved and impacted their lives. This is where you would include the four teenage grandchildren, the husband, etc. You will begin the list with "My family members that were Impacted by her/his death are." Then you will see that the list will end with a sentence that states "But I was(felt) alone, as I had no one when she/he died." Let's do that and then, I will give you your next steps. (I have a really large family so to prevent this from turning into a genealogy book I will only write my primary list):

"My Family Members that were impacted by her death are:

Papa Hale

Mike

Jaye

MJ

Junior

Michelle

Al

Brybry

Lee

Mae

Moe - (Me, yes this is what my family called me for years on end)

But I was (felt) alone, as I had no one when she/he died"

Now that you have written the lists, I want you to read it out loud from beginning to end. I want you to take a pause between each of their names and picture them in your thoughts. Allow it to resonate in your thoughts so you may begin to question if you truly were alone by choice or were you really alone. Some may be estranged from their family and that's ok, for now. So yes, this may be a hard task for you. The purpose of this exercise is for you to offset the disappointment of feeling alone in your grief because just as I have lost, I have nine siblings and a father at a minimum who lost as well. Meaning, they too were highly impacted by the same loss. The reality is that at least 10 other people were grieving the exact same person. Although circumstances didn't cater to it, we weren't alone and could have been positioned to have great success in a supportive atmosphere. I'm sure we can find commonality in how we feel to ease the stress of feeling alone. Although, yes, when you lay down at night it's just you, alone with your thoughts. Death has a way of intentionally, unintentionally isolating people. It eats away at your dignity and makes us feel that no one will recognize the pain we've endured. Who wants to talk about feelings and emotions, especially "dark" feelings and emotions? Grief is sort of an interesting topic. Everyone feels it at some point in their life but many are afraid or don't know how to speak about it.

If you want to take this exercise a little further I invite you to write next to each name a committed time and date in which you will call, text or meet for lunch with that person. I am sure that if you are troubled in your heart, I'm certain they are or may have felt it too. Did another family member react in a way where you felt a little worried about them? Maybe they were too quiet at the funeral. Did they suddenly stop calling you or maybe you don't hear from them as much? Here is your chance to help with your grief as well. Ask questions such as, how are they holding up, or give a hug, etc. If you haven't gotten it by now, allow me to spell it out for you. You are not meant to tackle grief on your own. It takes the support of family and friends. You have to keep reminding yourself that you are not alone. When you are starting to feel that way again take a look at the list of all the people that you, yourself wrote down and if you have the need to connect with one of them, do so immediately.

Show and Tell

Let's take a walk down memory lane to elementary school or even middle school where the famous show and tell project excited every student in the class. As it should, this was your moment to pick something from your home that you thought was amazing enough to share with a bunch of your classmates. Whatever artifact you chose, it had to be monumental as this was your golden opportunity to tell everyone how cool you are and show how cool your things are as well. So we knew it had to be good. Whether it was something of yours, or your sister's, or your mom's, or your dad's, whatever it was you cherished it. You put high regard on it enough to bring it to class, present to your classmates, write an essay and put together an A+ poster board for it. I'm sure you were proud of yourself and the artifact that you chose. Action step number three will take the same principles but for some of you, this will require you to dig deep within yourself to finally let go.

Are you still living in the same house in which your mother died? Do you have an entire shrine dedicated to your deceased father? Maybe you inherited all of your grandmother's things and now it has turned your home into an antique boutique? Or how about the room in which your beloved child once occupied that you walk by every day and so much as dares anyone to walk into without your permission? I want to know what you have and why you choose to keep those items. Here is what I want you to do. I want you to take an inventory of what you have that belongs to your deceased loved one, and I also want you to take an observation of where the items are located. If you want to take a picture and attach it to the journal entry, feel free to do that as well. Whatever it is, I want you to write down the reasons in which you keep them. I want you to think of the value it holds in your life, the memories in which it holds and the sentiment behind them. Now, this isn't something that I want you to get through quickly. This should be done based on the amount of stuff that you have. I want you to feel every piece. "Are you ready for Show and Tell class?" "Who would like to go first?" Morgan says, "I do teacher."

"Show and Tell

Nothing. Absolutely, positively, nothing. I have nothing that belongs to my mother. I also did not grow up with her things in the household, no pictures of her, no talk of her, nothing. I was certain she didn't exist. Or at least that's what they wanted me to believe. Not a single dress in sight, not a necklace to try on, not a ring to admire, no old furniture, no knick-knacks, nothing. When I say, nothing, I absolutely mean, nothing. Quite frankly this makes me sad to know that you died when I was barely 12 months and there is not a trace that you ever were a part of the family's life. Here I am as an adult with still nothing that was to be passed down. Did you have any belongings? At this point maybe you were a vagabond in which now I'm just being ridiculous for even thinking that. But what am I supposed to think as a child with no mom; when it's a crime to even think about you let alone speak your name in this household? What I do know is that whoever wanted me and my siblings to forget your existence, did a really good job. Now whoever is responsible for this, I'm unsure what their motives were, but they failed miserably. You are a very present force that surrounds all of your children. I get it now, when you died you became 10 times stronger to protect and guide all 10 of your children. But there must be something that belongs to you somewhere in the home, sorry to disappoint but that's a big fat nothing. However, I must say the closest thing that I have that reminds me of you is something that belonged to one of your brothers, which is my uncle. I remember it was when I was 1st being reintroduced to your side of the family by accident. By "accident," I mean your family began to show up in our lives by attending events that my older siblings, who were adults, decided to invite them to. I had no idea that they even existed. Their existence was just like yours, not really there but around. I was in high school and my eldest sister produced a play in which case debuted I believe sometime in April. Some of your siblings were there and a few of their children. I met a couple of your siblings, a pair of twin aunty and uncle. I thought it was interesting because of course I was a twin and anything that was a part of getting closer to know you, gave me a little anxiety. It just so happened that it was their birthday. As I was meeting them, although on the inside I was excited but anxious, I was very shy and a little guarded due to all the horror stories that I heard about your side of the family. I also didn't want there to be a conflict of interest once I got home if I showed too much interest and excitement in front of my dad and his wife. I knew things would get a little hostile when we got home. So I had to contain myself to show zero emotions when meeting them. "Hi Morgan, I am so happy to see you! Do you know who we are?" Said with a big smile from my uncle and a warm hug from my aunty. "No, I don't," I said, with my eldest sister watching from afar smiling and waiting for my reaction. "I am your Aunt and this is your Uncle, we are so glad to meet you!" As the conversation progressed I then learned it was their birthday and all of a sudden right before they left, he looked at me, took the necklace from around his neck and placed it around mine. "I want you to have this nephew," he said and then proceeded to hug me. At that moment, I did not react but I truly never felt close to knowing your existence in my life until that moment. So I may not have anything physical that belongs to you but I will always cherish that moment of you."

As you can see my show and tell project was different because as you have read, I do not have anything that belonged to my mother. Your story might be different as death and its effects are not the same for each individual. To this day I hold that necklace near and dear to my heart. Now that you have taken inventory of the material things that you have of your loved one, I want you to think for a moment the kind of emotional attachment that it has on you. I hope you didn't think that was the end of the exercise. Death is a traumatic experience and those who have experienced it indefinitely have something that belongs to that person and cherishes it as if it were gold. Holding on to a deceased person's possessions on a large scale can be detrimental to the healing process. I promise, you will never forget that person but having such a magnitude of items will keep you in the same place mentally and sometimes physically. So here is what I want you to write next. I want you to write a commitment to giving yourself a hard deadline in which you will remove the majority of the things from your possession.

That's right, it's time to let go of them. If you haven't touched the room in which they used to occupy, it's time to take that step. Again if you were gifted an entire household of things to only be transferred to your household where you now have two living room sets, occupying one family room, two ovens, two refrigerators, double the wardrobe, etc it's time to take that next step. This reminds me of the TV show series of Martin, the sitcom, where Martin and Gina first moved in together. Martin had his apartment, Gina had her apartment and of course, they both were fully furnished. However, when Gina moved in with Martin, of course, she thought her furnishings were better and as did Martin. The two get into a big argument over whose things to keep and who should get rid of their furnishings. Because they were both stubborn you see the next scene opening with two of everything in the small apartment. Gina is sitting on her sofa and Martin is sitting on his sofa ignoring each other. To this day it's a hilarious scene and I'm still wondering how they managed to get all that stuff in that tiny apartment!

Unfortunately, this isn't a sitcom with a crew working overtime to make good TV. This is real life and I know some of you are going through the same thing with real-life emotions. Let me make it clear. I am not saying that you should get rid of it all. Please do not trash everything as if your loved one did not exist. Hang on to a few reminders that allow them to continue to live. Although some people hang on to a few things others will hang on to large quantities, ultimately hanging on to the larger issue at hand. I want you to know that it is ok to let go of an entire room. I can't tell you what things to keep and what to let go of. I do have some options and questions to ask yourself that will help guide you on this journey. What are your thoughts surrounding putting the majority of it in storage? What about donating it to a place where you know it will go to god use or where your loved one volunteered? Is there a family member that would like to have some things? How about you tell the whole family that you will be opening your home for an artifact party for anyone to get a keepsake for themselves? Are there particular items that your loved one cared for the most? A favorite dress or suit? Maybe some jewelry? Do you have an attic or basement where those items can live boxed up and every now and again when it is storytime with your grandchildren or children or friends you pull out a few things? Is the house that was willed to you on its last leg but you're in denial as you want to keep it as is; just the way that grandma left it so you don't forget her and it stays in the family? Maybe it's time to renovate or sell? Again this does not mean that you have to do those things, and I can't make those decisions for you. Those questions are meant to guide you to make the decisions that you need to make, which is ultimately giving up those items that are holding you back and keeping your chosen gold.

Remember, gone doesn't mean forgotten and out of sight doesn't mean out of mind in this situation. The purpose of this exercise is to get you to clear the clutter that you have inadvertently placed upon yourself. You may not see it but I assure you that those around you are feeling the effects of it. Hanging on to these things can and will control your livelihood. Your reliance on those things to make you "happy" is only a crutch where you will never learn to walk on your own. The death of a loved one I like to say has attachment issues. Almost like a relationship. Have you ever been in a relationship with someone who is extremely codependent upon you and they have attached themselves to your right hip? You probably couldn't breathe. It's all nice and fluffy in the beginning as you are feeling like the only person in the world to them. Their whole world revolves around you, they want to know everything, want to be with you every second of the day and say all kinds of romantic things. You can't even go to the restroom alone. Admit it, you feel loved and wanted, don't you? I mean who doesn't want to feel like they are important to the person that they are in a relationship with. Overtime things take a turn for the worse where the questioning now becomes irritable, where every moment of the day you are expected to display your love and affection to the other person otherwise they will feel abandoned. Your plans with the girlfriends or the guy friends turn into an argument because you are expected to spend every waking moment with them. Those relationships typically don't last long and if they do, someone is likely miserable and or feels trapped and doesn't know how to end things. If lucky, the two will find a way to make it work and exist independently within the relationship. Just like there is hope for a toxic relationship, there is plenty of hope for you co depending on the possessions of your loved ones. It would be nice if this would be an easy feat, but this will be challenging for some of you. It's perfectly fine to let go and scale back, but you must move forward with the small gold that you have. Cherish that gold and allow it to be what you refer to as your success and strength.

These three action steps can play a crucial role in deepening your understanding of your grief and moving forward in it. To start with, getting things off your chest can be the difference in going insane to one day exploding or taking truth for what it is. Take power in knowing that you have control over your well being. Think of this step as a release where you dump everything you are feeling on paper. It has to come out or it will harm you. You must remember to be open and honest about everything. Now action step number two is a little different but takes it one step further in evaluating your current emotions surrounding a belief that no one gets it and that you are without a doubt all alone. This is a test that is birthed from death. It takes something from you that you care for so deeply and have invested so much into only to be let down in disappointment when they are gone. It's unfair. Realizing that your loved one was not only taken from you but from a collective group of people can make the world of difference on your journey. I am certain that you must have heard the saying "there is strength in numbers," and I truly believe that it does take a village. Including those close to you during your time of grief is super important. Allow them to be your backbone to help you stand tall in the face of adversity. You will need it and your relationships will prove to be a healthy force. Making those first two steps will lead you to make one more huge step and that's giving your loved one items an appraisal. How much is it worth to you? Now of course these items are priceless. Here is what I am asking. Is it worth losing your sanity? Have you lost all sense of normalcy that you used to have? Are the relationships with those living at wit's end because of the accumulation of items? Is it worth you losing your entire livelihood because you haven't dealt with the real problem at hand; that you are deeply hurting and just can't let go. I'm sure that you will find this exercise to be freeing just like the others. This is not the end-all to coping with the loss of a loved one. These are stepping blocks to help you along the way. Take them and apply them in your everyday bustle. When you find yourself reverting to those same things, take your journal and read your commitments to truly harness your true potential.

CHAPTER V

ROAD TO RECOVERY: THE COURAGE TO LIVE

On this long journey we call life, we will be faced with numerous blows to try and take us off the path that we were meant to travel. This task is even more difficult when we have lost the person that we believe was meant to travel the road with us. It's a stopping point which we believe will take us nowhere; we are indefinitely lost. The listed exercises above will allow you to begin to drive down this road again. It's time to get in the vehicle, put your seatbelt on, turn on that funky music, throw on those cool sunglasses and put your foot on the gas to drive. If you like, let the windows down or let the top back so you can feel the breeze on your skin. This is you. With the ambition and motive to move forward, you made the correct turn. Here's the thing at some point you will approach a red light, need a quick snack, then lunch, or maybe run out of gas. It happens and you know what, that's ok. Pullover, refill your tank, get a meal and keep going. This is how life works in general and when it comes to grief your burnout may happen at an alarming rate. I can hear you saying now (or maybe not), "I don't drink gas like a car, what do you mean by 'refill my tank'?" You've got questions and I've got answers. There are a few things that I think would help you refill your tank. Now, these are just a few options and by reading this, I hope that it will get your brains turning on what works for you.

To start with, it's important to just live. Allow me to explain what I mean by, live. You will need to be intentional about seizing every moment of your life and seeing the purpose and fulfillment each of those moments bring. As you are aware and have heard plenty of times, life is short. A cliche but true and relevant nonetheless. To live means, in its simplest form, seeing the beauty in walking your dog to spending quality time with family and friends. It means that when a good friend or associate invites you out for dessert tasting that you don't make an excuse to decline knowing that you will only be in your home trapped with your sorrow. Let me remind you to not find comfort in overindulging as an escape, but to indulge because you are taking control of the moment to enjoy a sweet treat. When you decide to live, you decide that you are going to get out of your way and take a chance on yourself. It means that when you see an attractive person that you say, hi, in an alluring way to make sure that there is no misunderstanding of interest. Allow yourself to live knowing that you are working on your best self and that who you are is a survivor. Begin to reshape how you see yourself living a life knowing that your loved one will be proud of you. It's about giving yourself the privilege of self-worth knowing that there is nothing that can stop you. So live. The next refill that any human suffering from grief can do is to seek additional help. This can come in many forms. One of these could be starting with your place of work. If you are finding that it's becoming increasingly challenging to deal with the pressure of work and your personal life, you should reach out to your human resources department and ask about the EAP, Employee Assistance Program. The EAP is a likely included benefit that came with your employment contract. At least that has been the case for me at all of my previous jobs. It's a program that is designed to give employees additional help for any personal or work-related problems that could affect not just your work performance but your mental and emotional well being. So start there. If you are not eligible for this benefit for some odd reason (most companies may even make exceptions for part-time staff if the need is dire, especially if you have tenure) the next thing to begin researching, are local grief counselors that will help you in your transition. I know, I know, for some cultures therapy or "seeing a shrink" has a negative association with it but I assure you that it would be of benefit to seek professional help. A few tips for you: Always be open and honest with your therapist, show up on time as there is no need to waste money and seek consultation if you are at wit's end. What do you have to lose? If you feel that that particular therapist isn't working, it's ok to look for another (it's not a one size fits all). However, you must trust the process and wholeheartedly participate. Let's say you can't afford a therapist at the moment. First, start saving, this is a true investment, but in the meantime a couple of low-cost options are A) look for a support group that you can attend. Yes, these do exist and are likely free. B) Begin to talk with someone in your circle about the issues you are having. Remember to talk with someone you trust. C) Look at what you are doing now. You're reading a book that was created to help people just like you and I. There are tons of books out there that you can purchase to lead and guide you to a more manageable life of grief.

A refill can take various forms, and another option is to take on a new hobby or reconnect with an old hobby that you once loved to do but no longer engage. Do you like to sew, read or maybe you love to travel? Did you used to love gardening but these days when you look out the window all you can see is a plant bed that has withered away? This is your time to bring new life into those old things. The circumstances behind giving that hobby up can vary, but let's breathe life into it again and this time put a spin on it. Do you grow the best roses in your garden or maybe you are on a mission to grow the largest watermelon? I am sure there is a contest for those types of things. Purchase the latest romantic thriller novel and join a book club. The good thing about those options is that you won't be alone as you will at some point meet with the group for a discussion of the book and eventually for the garden competition you will have a conference to attend where you will compete for the title. Use those moments to get to know some people. This could be a challenge for some, which leads me to my next refill option and that is to simply be open. That means don't discount things that are unfamiliar to you. Be open to new ideas and new people to enter your life. For example, if you have never been to the gym, this could be something that you can be open to trying. I promise it's not as intimidating as it may seem and not all gyms are the same. You could very well walk into one gym where it seems like everyone has been fit their entire life wherein one hand they are eating a raw broccoli head and in the other drinking a bottle of 4 uncooked eggs (if you see this run and don't turn back...I'm just kidding. It's ok to laugh here). Then you could visit another gym where the people are friendly and welcoming. Before you join, I recommend taking a tour and even asking if they have a trial session that you can take advantage of. The main objective is that you go into the gym with openness. Being open includes taking suggestions or advice that you may not consider yourself. Take into account that there may be a risk that comes along with this but I implore you to use your best judgment when they arise. I dare not say it, but adopting a new furry friend can very well fall into the category of trying something new. Now if you've already reached the max limit of animals in your home, feel free to leave this one to someone else. However, an animal companion can be a great addition to the family that can assist. If you love pets but don't want or can't afford to have one present in your life, don't worry. Search for nearby groups that have trained dogs to relieve stress in humans. These groups often visit libraries, college campuses, etc. Feel free to show up to pet a dog or two and continue with your day. This is a win-win situation. I mean seriously, what dog will turn down a good belly rub and all that attention, not a single one. In return, you have an opportunity to experience the joy that becomes contagious. There is something about the happiness of a dog that is transferred to humans in interaction. Cherish that moment and don't let it go. Openness is a state of mind that you will have to work at. We as humans are used to what we know and what traditionally has worked for us in the past but remember it's a new day so give yourself the gift of openness.

There are two more refills that I want you to consider. My hard goal is to give you options after options in dealing with your grief. I want to leave nothing off the table although I fear I will. My intentions are for you to have something as a baseline versus starting from nothing. With the idea that many are lost in their grief, allow these refills to guide you down this road to recovery. Have you considered volunteering? Hear me out now. This refill option is one that keeps on giving. Volunteering is a great way to give back to yourself and others. The gratitude that comes from this is unmatchable to know that you have just invested either your time or talent for something that affects a large community of people who will one day grow up to do the same for the next person. When volunteering, I don't want you to randomly choose. If you are afraid of animals, then it's probably not best for you to volunteer at your local zoo. Just as if you know your patience level is at an all-time low, you walk extremely fast and typically rush elderly people when they are walking in front of you, you might not be best suited for volunteering at a senior citizens center. This will involve you digging deep within yourself to seek a true understanding of what issues highly affect you. Where do you want to make a change? Perhaps the issues don't affect you personally; maybe you just have a soft spot for certain causes. Typically people join causes because they were impacted in some way by the mission. This is good in that you want to be a part of something that interests you and even affects you on an emotional level. You will likely be more involved and can truly refill your passion in life.

The last refill option, but certainly not the least, that I want to bring to your attention (because I am sure there are plenty more) is to dig deeper into your faith. Losing a loved one is rough times from the most vulnerable to the strongest. So rough, that sometimes we curse God and our faith out of the anger, pain and sorrow that we have just experienced. We ask, God, "Why did this happen to me? You should have taken me instead." This is especially true in situations where it was completely unexpected due to a homicide, suicide, freak accident, etc. (If you remember from chapter one we discussed the notion that death and life do not discriminate and the placement of blame). Having this understanding will allow you to shift your focus and energy in making decisions that will help you to grow. Death and life are natural things that occur in the course of creation. By our measures we could say "it was too soon" but who are we to decide what's too soon. Once you come around to yourself you will be able to recognize that all things work together for good. Some give up though. You have to keep fighting for your sanity. The things that you will experience in life are unexplained and unplanned. Who knew that you would lose your job at 40 where you've been faithful to the organization for the past 20 years. Vice versa, who knew that in the same job someone who started at the same time as you will be promoted to your superior. Life is strange, but I have found that digging deeper into my faith in God has allowed me to find peace knowing that death in any form is an equilibrium of the human race. If you are like me this is comforting news because if you look up the definition of a control freak, I'm almost certain that you will see my picture. Being a control freak made me anxious beyond belief. It messed with my self-confidence and ultimately catered to a series of bad sleeping habits which resulted in a self- diagnoses of insomnia for a good amount of my early and mid-twenties. Refills, refills, refills. Find what works for you. Be open to trying something new or different. As you see there are plenty of options for you, so feel free to explore and get going again.

On your new journey, you will need the courage to live as problems arise. It can be a scary road. The "unknown" is a place that makes certain people uneasy. Facing the hard truth of losing a loved one can have this effect where your entire life will flash right before your eyes. It's common that once a loved one dies, people often wonder, how will they move on from this; is it possible to move forward? Sometimes we lose faith, all hope and completely call the game. It's important to understand that life goes on and you must make a choice to keep pedaling. I am sure it is what they would want you to do. When such events happen a part of us dies as well. The heart takes a major blow which destroys confidence, courage, worth and the ability to love again. If it doesn't destroy it rest assured it will penetrate it in some form or fashion. We will never understand why death took from "me." We go through many emotions as you start to try and imagine life without them. Sometimes you just can't imagine it. It's too painful to think of. For our next exercise, I want you to write down every major event that happened in your life and any upcoming events since the passing of your loved one. Whether it be good or bad, write it down. I want you to take your time on this one. There is absolutely no rush. This will require you to think for a while, so while you are thinking, allow me.

Events that have happened to me since your passage:

- *My 2nd birthday through the rest of my life.*
- *When I got expelled from preschool.*
- *1st day of kindergarten*

- *When I learned how to ride a bike*
- *When I was expelled in middle school*
- *My sweet 16.*
- *When I became class president in high school*
- *My 1st track meet*
- *I became a Jr. Attorney in the criminal justice program and you missed my first trial, (I sentenced the defendant to 1300 hours of community service)*
- *The day I had to put a pause on the running track in high school because the doctor found an imbalance in my heartbeat rhythm. He said that I had a heart murmur (looks like you left me another gift). I was so afraid, mom.*
- *Missed my prom - I wore all white with a silver tie and vest, very sharp for my standards.*
- *My high school graduation- At graduation, I sang the class song in front of thousands. This was the first time that I sang with my family listening. They had no idea that I could sing. Later on, I found out that dad was pretty stoked about it.*
- *College move-in day - I had no one mom but the twin you gifted me with.*
- *The day I was initiated into a college fraternity.*
- *When I began dating (I could have used your advice)*
- *When I graduated from college. This was probably one of the worst times in my life. It should have been a celebration but it wasn't.*

- *When I bought my first car*
- *The day I moved into my 1st apartment.*
- *My first time on an airplane*
- *Hurricane seasons*
- *The day I lost my job.*

But some things haven't happened yet that you will miss as well, mom

- *The day I will get married*
- *My first child and all after.*
- *My first home purchase*
- *More Christmas' and thanksgivings*
- *and all the unknown*

This list can go on and on for my individual life. It goes without being said that a lifetime of events has passed where I had to live through, without my loved one. The second part of this exercise after you have written all the events, is I want you to read out loud the entire list of major events that have happened in your life. You will start your sentence off by saying "These are the events that meant so much to me." When you get to the very end of the list, you will end it with "and you weren't there." Don't worry you can find extracted journal instructions and the end of this book. I want you to read that aloud until it resonates with the emptiness that you are longing to fill. I want you to think of the weight that each of those events carries in your life. The events you chose to write down have significance to you. Otherwise, you would not have written them down. Now that you have realized that your loved one wasn't present for past events, what about future events? Will he or she be at those events? Of course, the answer to that is, no. The goal here to recognize the past as a learning opportunity and prepare for the future. It's nothing like being disappointed over and over again because your spouse has cheated on you for the 3rd time to only find yourself shocked when you find out for the 4th time that he or she has been unfaithful (I hate to say it but it happens). By this time, you either have moved on or you have lowered your expectations of your partner and aren't completely caught off guard for the disappointment. Or say you have a check-up with the doctor and he says, "You need to change your eating habits or you could develop diabetes." Then down the line a few years later you haven't changed anything about your diet and the doctor tells you that you have diabetes. You were privy to the signs and information beforehand to prepare for this. How about your mom calling you on the way home to take the frozen meal out the freezer to soak in water to thaw. Only you didn't. You believed you had the time and now mom is home and everyone is disappointed because you failed to prepare for dinner. This is the same concept. You have to prepare now for the future when it comes to having relief in your grief. Now, this isn't to say that your future events won't be emotional for you. This is to give you the courage to acknowledge your sadness and position the emotion to be controlled most healthily.

How do we find the courage to move on to the next major event? The simplest answer that I can offer you is acceptance. "How do I move forward?" The question that we all face. We must learn to accept uncontrollable fates, release control and set your minds free. However, let's not confuse acceptance with exclusion. They do not compliment each other and are not synonymous. Your loved one will forever be a part of you. Trust me, I know these events will be overwhelming without your loved one. Life will never be the same without them and although they weren't and will not be there physically, you have the privilege of seeing that your loved one is represented. Remember, we want to see that we welcome our deceased loved ones in our lives sustainably and healthily. We want to contribute small but meaningful things. For example, births. Is it possible to name the child after your loved one to honor them? If you are scheduled to get married and your mom or dad won't be present, could you repurpose their old dress or old tux to wear; incorporate it into your clothing somehow. Better yet match the color scheme to their favorite or get married at a significant destination or landmark connected to them.

Just as we talked about before, the next thing is to be free in your remembrance of them. It's ok to remember them. This falls right in line with welcoming them into life events where sometimes we feel that we must suppress remembering our loved one to move forward. We also dare not mention them due to "keeping the peace" amongst the family. When your loved one shows up as a thought to you, you must make a conscious effort to do two things and that's lean into those thoughts while controlling the emotion surrounding it. You are to lean into those thoughts as a moment of reverence. Reverence for your loved one and reverence for yourself. This is reverence for yourself, you see, because in our grief is where we will be able to truly activate our true courage and true self. Each time this happens, you will honor it as a moment of reflection and move forward to release a strength that you never thought you possessed. Some people believe that there is a weakness that comes from grief and however, it is the exact opposite; an unstoppable strength that is ready to blossom in you.

After you've done those two things, do me a favor and do two more. This will be fun I promise you. I want you to sing. You read it right the first time. I want you to sing like nobody's listening and belt out those notes like the famous Celine Dion or Whitney Houston. Better yet how about John Legend or Prince. When you find yourself feeling a little sad, you can either decide that you want to sing your loved one's favorite song or be a wild card and sing whatever makes you happy. If you haven't heard, singing is known to release endorphins, ie, a natural antidepressant. It has proven to have significant benefits on lowering stress levels and improves your mental alertness; helping you develop your concentration and memory. So whether you want to join a choir, take private singing lessons or do it the old fashion way and sing completely off-key in the echo of your shower, know that you have a number one fan and that's me. Now the second thing is something that often compliments singing and that is the good old fashion two-step. (I've never learned the two-step, by the way, that was before my time). I want you to dance. Either to the beat or not. Who cares the main thing here is that you need to get moving to intentionally change your current mindset. I've found it true in life that you can't do one without the other. What's peanut butter without jelly, cereal without milk, tea without lemon and a song without a dance. It's almost an offense to all the amazing pairs of our lifetime. No ones asking you to be perfect like the Alvin Ailey Dance Company. Your goal is to take this time back for yourself. When emotion fills us, sometimes it can overtake us. It doesn't happen all at once either for some folks. It starts slowly picking at you day by day and then we find ourselves by the end of the week feeling horrible. Some people may need to dance and sing every day to break habits of unhealthy thoughts, just as some people may need to see a therapist more often than not. Eventually, you will see that you can slowly start to take back your life and emotional being. Remember you have a lifetime to go so you must take the time to fully process everything that you are feeling.

Let's keep moving. To move forward in your grief, I want to share with you the next steps you'll need to take. When you lose a loved one that you were deeply rooted in, this change can have such a devastating impact. Think about it. Similar to a tree. If you uproot a tree it will die eventually as it isn't getting any nutrients or even water. The leaves will wither away, the branches will rot and will be turned into paper, possibly wood to build a house, a chair, shavings for a farm, pencils, paper and the list can go on. The tree died and was repurposed into many different objects in life, which means that it served its purpose alive and will live on again in a second life. Just as the tree went on to provide an additional purpose in someone else's life, the same applies to your loved one's death. The tree will no longer provide shade and of course the main purpose of creating air for us as humans to live and breathe, it serves the purpose just as well as the 1st. Live life knowing that the life and death of your loved one were for a reason beyond any reasoning you may think of. Therefore you must grant yourself the right to grieve and stop trying to make sense of it. That should go without saying, right? Giving yourself the freedom to grieve can be the difference between letting a rotten tree fall on you or deciding to move out of the way. The sadness can and will hit you hard. It's no joke. Yes, it's as serious as choosing to live. Here's a tip which we have covered before; suppressing is not the act of granting yourself the right to grieve. It's a form of avoidance and denial that will set a fuse sooner or later. You may find yourself so good at ignoring it that you began to ignore every other emotion that you feel. Like showing happiness or joy at your seven-year-olds basketball game. What about when you're in a conversation with a friend and you misinterpret their reality for something negative towards you? The worst of it all is you're living life not showing love and compassion for anyone around you. The reason; you forgot to acknowledge the hurt and pain that has festered in you and now it has completely taken control of your entire being. Life is hard enough and for you, it may be even harder now. You lost a loved one. Take this moment and live in it to discover the 2nd life that your loved one will hold in your life. How will the death and life of your loved one be repurposed? Whether in your personal life or with a sibling that has yet to come to terms with the death. Maybe that's you passing on a legacy to your children through storytelling, a recipe, or a tradition; because guess what, dead and gone, doesn't mean that you bury every ounce of meaning that you once shared.

In this process of overcoming your grief, I want you to find your voice. Grief-stricken people are almost forced into the idea that who we are, have died right alongside our loved one. For plenty, this is immense, where depending on the circumstances surrounding the death, you may have been a pillar to that person or that person was a pillar to you. Such as an ongoing battle with heart disease or cancer. Maybe you were an only child or the "favorite" child. Regardless of the circumstance, when your loved one died, a lot of things died with them. The physical love and support they would give, the advice they would give and with growing pains you'll miss out on the future wisdom and knowledge that they would be able to share. This doesn't mean that you stop finding your way. This means that you continue with knowing two things. A) I have previous memories that I can refer to when I need advice and B.) You will use that to fuel your future self. Allow the wisdom and love that they once shared with you to be the foundation in which you build yourself to discover your voice, your purpose and your heart's desires in life. Finding your voice means that you must find out who you can become without them. Finding your voice will challenge the courage to be authentically, uniquely you in every way. Your voice doesn't diminish when your loved one dies, it amplifies it. Your voice is rooted in your loved one but now it's time for it to sprout realizing that the root will always be there. It's the sustainer and foundation of your life.

CHAPTER VI

A DREAM COME TRUE

Those dealing with grief sometimes can't begin to fathom a life worth dreaming of. Our wants and needs are a bit different from those around us. Our American Dream is altered a little bit. Before things changed (the death of our loved one) we imagined our future selves, who we wanted to be, how we planned to live, the spouse we wanted to marry, the children we wanted to bare, the house we wanted to move into, the car we wanted to drive and the island we wanted to visit. All of that shifted the moment we found out that one of our most favorite people in the world has died. This isn't to say that we stopped working towards a better life for ourselves, but in that moment and moments to follow the only thing that we were interested in, is hearing and seeing our loved one just one more time. This one time will take away the pain, the fears, the uncertainty and confusion. We want and wanted it so badly that we would do anything and I mean anything, to experience the warmth of our loved one. It would allow us to keep living for even just a minute at that moment. These moments are crucial to us in that we want to know that we are on the right track. If I am unable to hear your voice or see your face, show yourself to me in any form. That's our heart's desire.

I remember very vividly the very first moment my mother appeared to me. Let me remind you that her death came very suddenly for her at an early age where her youngest children were barely walking and not potty trained. Needless to say, her face and voice were extremely unfamiliar to me even as a young adult. As you have read early on, the month leading up to my scheduled graduation from college was a challenging time for me. Fast forward a couple of months later, I moved in with my older brother. One day, it was about 6 pm, I was alone in his home and it's not quite dawn just yet. As I was taking a nap on the sofa, in the upstairs den, a dream had overtaken me. This dream, I will never forget. The dream, oddly enough, featured three people. My mom, my step-mother, and I. Strange, right? The dream started with my step-mother in the background. She was behind the sofa focused on ironing. She never looked up or said anything. Just ironing. Then all of a sudden, in the same room at the same time my mother appeared and she was sitting on the sofa smiling watching me on the floor. I appeared to be about five to seven years of age. I had her obituary in my hand fiddling with it. I wasn't looking at her and if sadness was a person, it would have been me in that dream as a child. While still smiling and looking at me she turns to my step-mother, who is still focused on ironing, and says, "Awww he's upset and sad." My mom then turns to me and asks, "What's that you have in your hand? Is that an obit, obit, obit...?" She struggled to say that word, I then quickly interrupted and corrected her by saying "It's an obituary." I said it in a confused way, like, "You don't know how to pronounce that word?" I thought. Then looked at her in the corner of my eyes, like "are you kidding me?" (I was a smart-alit as a child, pretty smart beyond my years, so this makes perfect sense). After that, she smiled in her proudness of me and folded her hands on her lap. Just like that the dream was over with me instantly waking up with my heart racing and tears falling down my eyes at a rapid pace. I was in a panic and could not open my eyes as I had no control over my crying. I was truly upset that it was over yet afraid of what I had just experienced. This was the very first time that I heard my mother's voice. She spoke to me and touched my heart. Me! I had no doubt that it was her face and that she was who she was. Then all of a sudden, in my wailing weeping, I started to laugh with joy and it wasn't because I heard her voice or saw her face. It was because of the joke she made. You see her "pretending" to act like she didn't know how to pronounce the word "obituary" in the dream was her way of showing her love towards me by implying that, "Yes I know you, my son. Although I am not physically there with you I am watching over you." She knew that I would be a "smarty pants" and correct her in the dream. She also knew that once I was awake and aware that I would be in sorrow and that joke would be something to make me laugh to bring me back to life.

That dream gave me life to move forward and to grant myself the privilege of being me. You see dreams do come true. Whether you believe in the supernatural or not. Know that this was my experience and that every experience won't be that same. Your loved ones won't appear to you in the same way or maybe they will. We spoke about this early on in the book; about how you should be open to different experiences to allow your loved ones to be revealed. I won't go through that again but refer to chapter five to get the inside scoop. This chapter, I want to bring to your attention the steps of what it means to have dreams come true and that is the sole act of reaching that point of pure euphoria. A true feeling or state of intense excitement and happiness that requires no regret. It's about you and always have been if you haven't gotten the message thus far. I want you to be happy, filled with joy and purpose building the person you always wanted to be. This will require you to do a little bit of work that will ask for your persistence. This isn't to say that you won't get tired and need a physical or mental break. We all do, and when you feel that you need a break, take it! Go back to chapter five and read all about how you too, can refill your tank. No one's tank stays full. It requires a little bit of maintenance. It's going to require you to hold yourself accountable even when no one else will. This dream come true is you; one step closer and fully capable of turning a tough situation into a triumphant victory. You probably guessed where this is going by now and you've guessed right. There is one last activity that I want us to do together and of course, in true fashion, I'll go first. It's time to commit to doing the necessary work to overcome your grief and activate the potential that is screaming to be released. For this exercise, I want you to think of all the things that you love, and love doing. What are you best at? What makes you, YOU? Think of the things that make you, say "that's totally me," or maybe just simply write what you have learned about yourself during this journaling process. This will begin with "What about me..." and end with "These are the things I love"

"*What about me...*

Let me take a moment here, sometimes I'm not too sure what I love doing. Everything that I thought I loved was only for the approval of someone else. I ran track because I thought it would make my dad more involved with my life just as he did for the other brothers. I was actually really good at it but that didn't get me what I was looking for and I didn't care too much about it. I stuck with it because I was good at it. Let's see, what do I love?? Hmmm. This is tough for me as exploring my likes and dislikes didn't come easy for me. What I can say is that, if anything, I've learned that I am comfortable being me and that I have never felt safer in my life. I know that my mother's death wasn't for nothing and although I miss her dearly, I know that her love lives on through me. It's funny how things work. Losing her has helped me in finding myself and I am forever grateful. I know that I have a lifetime to go on this journey. Each day I will learn to love even just the smallest of one more thing about me. Like my voice. I was gifted with a singing voice that I love to utilize. Do you know what else I love? I love how welcoming and accepting I am to people. Some may see this as a curse but my thoughts are that we are all just one flight away from our next breakthrough. I see others with no presumptions and I love that because people get to be free around me. This may seem small but I also love the little birthmark that is on my face. For a long time as a child, I wondered why it was there and honestly thought that only women had the privilege of having birthmarks. That just seems silly. Man oh man, I love my family as well. They too have been through hell and back and I'm surprised we are still standing. I love going shopping and buying new pieces to fit in my wardrobe. In addition to shopping, I have a good eye for good style. I'm not a stylist though but I can direct you and make you feel good about your choices. I love meeting new people. I'm a true ambivert (although I'd like to believe I'm an introvert). Morgan, you are doing great buddy and I love you the most. Don't be so hard on yourself, you are still getting to know you. I am committed to making you, be the best you, I can by continuing to explode through different challenges and circumstances. I know you are not finished and there may be more but, these are the things I love.``

Leave it all on the paper and if you think of more, don't be afraid to go back and add it, because this is it. This is your moment to take the things that you have learned and apply them to your daily living. Turning those deepest darkest moments into wins that no one can stop. It's important to understand that although I (we) have lost, I (we) have also gained. My personal belief is that I have gained an angel to watch over me and more importantly I've gained a new perspective on life knowing that everyone and every day should be cherished. Your gain will look different than mine or it may look similar. Either way, that's up for interpretation, but make sure that your gain is always a step in the positive direction. This is all about you and the uprising in your grief. I hope that this exercise will permit those grieving to give yourselves the push you need to charge yourself with the work of taking charge of your life. Allow yourself to be led by your intuition to gain the support that is needed to move forward. During this process, if you are feeling lost and don't quite know where to start, ask yourself four questions:

1. What do you want?

2. What do you think your deceased loved one would say to you in regards to that?

3. Is what you want possible?

4. What are a few things that will help me attain it?

After you have asked yourself those questions, your next followup is to take action. Some people wonder "How do I get started?" The answer is this: You've already started by reading and being 100% vulnerable in your exercises. So smile at yourself. You start with one foot at a time so don't be afraid to start small. I know sometimes in the human race we feel that we aren't taking a risk if we don't jump big, but I beg to differ. You must learn to float before you learn to swim and soon you'll be just like Michael Phelps. But of course, I have suggestions for you. Three categories that I want you to implement into your life are activities surrounding the mind, body and soul. One of which you have already started, but let's start with my favorite, the body. As you know your body is a one time gift and as much, we should treat it that way. I'm not talking about the gift that you received as a child. That's temperamental and temporary. I'm talking about one of the precious gifts that life gives us. With this body, let's make it the best body ever because (everybody say it in unison) when you feel good you look good and for me that starts from a medical and physical standpoint. Trust me on this, you'd want to start by changing your eating habits. The foods you eat can either put you in a sluggish bad mood or it can boost your energy and put a skip in your step. In a world where a heavy steak can have you out cold for an hour or two versus a fresh homemade power-bowl that will grant you complete satisfaction for the whole day, I'm confident that my bet on the power-bowl will win every time. You can either have food curse your life or you can have it bless you in many ways. So many diseases and illnesses can be prevented by having a clear line of what goes into your system. Diabetes and Heart disease being two of those. I, myself, have chosen to go vegan and have been for a long time now. Several benefits come with being vegan and having healthy eating habits. Be strict on yourself. I've found that the food that I eat contributes to great headspace, (I'm almost certain you have heard of brain food).

The next practice that I want you to consider is a healthy mind. Since we know that the food you eat contributes to the actual health of your brain, another piece that will aid in the process is to see that you become sharper and sharper each day. This could start by doing something simple with a big impact, like reading aloud. If you haven't heard, reading aloud can increase your vocabulary as it forces you to sound about syllables for correct pronunciation. You should have been reading aloud all the exercises you have done thus far. Also, it will help with understanding text and helps to increase your long term memory. The mind is a very complicated system to understand and when it comes to your mind, your goal is to do something that keeps it stimulated. Complete a sudoku chart, how about a crossword puzzle, or make it a point to learn a new word and definition a day. Some people opt to learn a new language or learn to play an instrument. As I said, these are just small things that make a huge impact. If you want to get your mind going, may I suggest you buckle down and learn something new in your career field? You should be working to become an expert at what you do. This could include you taking 30 minutes each day solely focused on studying and improving your skill set. This will give you the confidence you need at work and can become a true asset to the team. Overall, become a true wealth of knowledge. The last thing I want you to take time for is your soul, which I believe is the sum of all wellness. Without a healthy and thriving soul, life can be a huge issue. The good thing is that you've already started one thing and that is journaling. Journaling helps you to release the soul of any issues that may be weighing it down. Our souls were meant to shine and with tar that death leaves behind it seek to take that away. Journaling will assist in decluttering your mind and release you from an overwhelming amount of thoughts. This will help you organize your feelings and help you to better express them to your loved ones when needed. Just as your body and mind are complex that benefits from multiple faucets, so is your soul. Make this nice and easy as you will need to place your soul at ease so it can be free to guide you. If that means you take a stretch and release group exercise class, then do it. If you need to take a walk in the park or along the beach, then do it, and my personal favorite if you need to have a massage, then do that too. While you're at it take a friend along that walk or class to increase the social aspect of the activity. Sometimes that can be even more draining, believe me, I know. So if you have a few close friends, get together for a good time that all of you can enjoy. Whether that's meeting up for tea or video calling your best friend to chat, have at it. Sometimes you don't have to go far from the home as your best friend could be right in the home with you (wink, wink); your spouse! A lot of times couples may forget that they can have fun with their significant other during this time. Be open and be honest but most of all take the strings off and relax. These three things will allow you to approach your individual life of grief with true desire and purpose.

Parents, guardians, and future parents alike, while attempting your "dream come true" purpose in life, you must strongly take into consideration how this will affect your children. You must include your children during this process as I have mentioned countless times, your children are, too, experiencing grief. They need you. A dream come true for you is nothing if your children are suffering day by day wondering hopelessly. Children are the most vulnerable human beings and for that reason, we must do our due diligence in protecting them at all costs. During this transition as a parent, you will need to take action on providing a few things for your children. Number one, your children will need to be nourished. I know you have heard that word and have used it on multiple occasions but have you taken the time to define and understand what it means? Let's take a look. Nourished in the Merriam-Webster Dictionary is defined; To Nurture, rear, to promote the growth of, to furnish or sustain with nutriment: Feed, Maintain, support. I support this definition completely because it is so multi-faceted in its approach to the realization of what is needed. You have the privilege of raising children and helping them with their "dream come true." "They" always say the way to a man's heart is with food, but as you see here in this definition the same goes for children. Feeding your children a healthy well-balanced meal with the proper nutrients is vital to their success. If you don't believe me, think about yourself for a moment. Whenever you get hungry and haven't eaten in a while how do you react? I'm sure you are likely irritable, can't get any work done because you have no energy and are very lethargic. Some are likely to turn into angry fire ants; biting everything that gets in the way. I'm sure your brainpower isn't at its fullest. There is no difference when it comes to children. Yes, their stomachs are a lot smaller but it must be filled with delicious food by all means. If you want your children to succeed, let's start there. Then keep moving because also a part of proper nourishment, you must promote growth with support and maintain that. In other words, stop limiting your children. That includes their voice as well. You have to be there for them and encourage them along the way. They will make mistakes along the way and you will be right there to help them work through what they have just experienced. They will thank you for this later but you must maintain this type of new attitude. It's needed because guess what children can sense when mom or dad has withdrawn from them. For a child to sense this type of behavior you can guarantee that some of them will react in many different ways. You can do this. I have the greatest faith in you.

The next action that is important that you must provide is "El-Oh-Vee-E" and what does that spell? That spells, Love. If you notice, I use the word "must." These actions are not optional. Fortunately, they are required. I know that perfectionism isn't possible and I'm not implying that you become perfect, but here's the thing: none of us are and we all make mistakes. What we do is that we pick up, learn from it and move on to the next day better than we were yesterday. I'm sure you have your definition of love but let's take a look at the official meaning. Love - Unselfish loyal and benevolent concern for the good of another, an assurance of affection, warm attachment, enthusiasm, or devotion. The first thing to understand is that you have to give of yourself. It's going to require you to see your children for who they are and to give them a piece of your heart so he or she is confirmed in knowing that they have someone on their side. You can't just show and even say I love you once every year and expect your child to have complete confidence in you. It has to be consistent through both your actions and how you react to them. I remember the first time my father said "I Love you." It was my sophomore year in high school, so about 16 years old. The family was going on a road trip to Tennessee but the younger children were going to stay back, as we had school. We weren't going. We were going to be staying at my grandmother's house. The night they were scheduled to leave, I put my things into my brother's car as he was going to be the one to take my twin sister and me to grandmas. As my sister and I left the house and walked outside, our dad followed us out. Everyone else stayed inside. My brother was already in the car waiting for the two of us, and I guess dad wanted to say goodbye one more time. So he did. After he said, "good-bye, you all be safe" he proceeded to say one more thing to us together. He said "I Love You" to my sister and I. My sister said, "I love you too." Do you want to know what I said? Now, don't laugh but I said, "OK" with no emotion, then went to my brother's car. This was the first time in 16 years that I heard my dad say those words. Let alone to me. Now culturally for his generation, that's unheard of to say as a man. At least that is what I have concluded. I was totally confused and shocked. So many thoughts went through my head. "What did he mean by that." "Does he mean that or is he just playing a trick on us?" "Why was my sister able to say it so quickly and not me?" "Has he said it to her before?" "Why hasn't he said it to me before?" "Surely he must have hated me before?" "It can't be real." "Can it be real?" "I've never thought about him loving me." "Why would he say that, now, after all these years?" "Did someone force him to say that?" "Did he only say it because I was with my twin?" "Was it even for me?" "Maybe, it was for her, and because I was walking with her, I just happened to hear it?" Yeah, he only said it to apply for my sister." "There's no way he meant it for me." I just could not comprehend his exact intentions and for the rest of the time that they were away on that trip it messed with my mind, then I started to feel horrible because I didn't say it back. It's one thing to know for certain that your child knows that he or she is loved by you vs having to go through so many emotions as I did to tassel and try to figure out if they are loved are not. Your role as a parent is to see that your child is secure in you and sees you as their s/ hero with no doubt about it. Remember to show it and say it, often.

It's all about your actions parents. Your babies (yes, this includes your newborn to your 30-year-old daughter or son) are watching you. Your actions are very visible to them. They may not physically and emotionally be able to understand but I assure you they will question you. It's crazy how a child's life is hinged on every decision a parent makes. This is why perseverance is the next action you must take. Perseverance sounds great to use when trying to get someone to overcome and here's why. Perseverance is defined as a continued effort to do or achieve something despite difficulties, failure, or opposition. The action or condition or an instance of preserving. This shouldn't come as a surprise that you would need perseverance, right? I have mentioned over and over again that this process is probably one of the hardest things that you will go through and at the first sign of difficulty, you have a choice to make. Will you uphold perseverance or not? Your children need to see you push past the obstacles and opposition so you can continue to help them do the same. One parent has died, they don't need the second one to die mentally. They need you alive and well. If one thing doesn't work, try something else. It's ok to try different methods. Some people try different partners, different outfits or maybe you didn't like a particular meal. For a long time, I hated fish as a teenager (back when I consumed meat). All of my friends and family were certain that I just didn't know what "good fish" tasted like. So every time we went out to eat or someone cooked they always said you should try this type or try it the way that I cook it. It was honestly shameful now that I think about it. The results, as you have read, I'm vegan now. I hated them all. However, I kept trying different things until I found what works for my appetite and voila, I'm feeling better than ever. I say that to say, not only to keep going but to keep going even in your discomfort. This will allow you to be stronger than ever and that's what your child needs. Believe it or not, they need you more than ever at this point and you need them. By doing this you will instill in your children the spirit of a warrior. A child that will grow to continue to fight and win. Can you imagine your child being unstoppable, unafraid all because they were influenced by you?

Another thing that is just as important as those above, is your faith. This concept can go a few different ways. Faith is what ties all of this together. The word faith is defined in many ways, and part of the definition states it is something that is believed especially with strong conviction. If you don't do anything else, believe in yourself. Simply have faith that you can and will. This requires a deeper thought process as you see because sometimes having faith means that there is no particular evidence to be seen. This is why "faith" doesn't work well in the court system as they have to have hard evidence to convict someone of a crime. Faith will require you to look within yourself and ask, "What do I believe?" Although I'm in pain trying to work through it, I don't seem to see anything new happening. It's almost like going to the gym when you are trying to lose weight. Some people lose faith in their abilities because they don't see the immediate results when they look in the mirror or step on the scale after a week's worth of exercising. It doesn't work that way. You have to have a strong connection with yourself. Yes, your children need you to believe in yourself. This may sound strange at first and I'm sure your children won't be able to verbalize this to you, however, when you display a high level of hopefulness for your children, it makes the world for them. All this to give your children the world you brought them into. Your role is to give them the necessary tools needed during this time to strengthen their minds and release them of any wall-building thoughts. Share stories with them so they don't have to "create" any of their own. Don't shy away from this either. Permit yourself so you may permit your children. They too deserve a dream come true.

This is your opportunity to create a new life. One that owes it to yourself to keep living. Take this time to truly put into practice the things that you have learned. The death of a loved one can indefinitely birth a new you.

CONCLUSION

Welcome to your beginning. No, we're not going to start from the front but rather this is your beginning to a brighter now. If you notice, I didn't say a "brighter future" or a "brighter tomorrow." In reality, we want our futures to be bright. It's always about tomorrow and the "now " is typically neglected. Your "now" will determine if you will have a brighter tomorrow or future. For plenty, tomorrow never comes. We get caught in the swarm of life and become exhausted before you even realize it. For your next phase in life, we should cherish the present, honor your past and be excited about the future. I'm going to tell you exactly what I mean by that.

Cherish the Present

In life, the present is what we have. It is the link that connects us to our future and without cherishing it we leave ourselves as vulnerable prey. Cherishing the now is something that will take practice. We are wired to worry about the future. What am I going to eat, what am I going to wear, what elementary school will my two-year-old attend in three years, etc. Let's face it, we have a lot on our plates and we are trying to gobble it all down by ourselves, really quickly and without actually savoring the taste. While you are scarfing it down, I'm sure someone has added something to it, if you didn't already add more. Slow down every now and again, more often. If not, you could miss your five-year-olds winning shot or you may miss the principal of the school calling your child's name at their high school graduation. There is something important about the now and you have to pause and ask, "What is this moment trying to give me?" "How can I make the most of this "now" that I am living through?" The present won't come again and you might end up living life in regret for the opportunity missed. As you have either already experienced and will experience, our loved ones are only with us for a short period, so take that present moment and live in it.

Honor Your Past

Sometimes in order to keep moving forward, we have to honor our past. That is, the experience that you have to pull from that has created the present you. It could be anything. Honoring those that have paved the way for you such as your family, honoring the choices that you have made up until this point in your life. Those that have come before, seek their knowledge and wisdom. They will have a lot to share. You may not agree with it all but that's ok. Your job is to receive it with open arms and decipher what makes sense to you for your family. Honoring your past allows you to halt bad habits and curses because it allows you to study the patterns and learn from the mistakes. Ultimately reinventing the future (which we will get to momentarily). Honoring your past means to accept the decisions that you have made and live knowing that it isn't a defining action unless you allow it to be. Everyone's past is relevant to each of our lives and this allows you to be free of any constraint that may be lingering from it. In our lives, we will have a combination of good and bad past choices. Take the good and run with it. Deal with the bad and leave it in the past. Let me refresh your memory; this is the beginning of everything that you wish could be possible and you won't be needing any extra baggage...unless you want to pay the extra fee (and who wants to pay extra fees, literally no one).

Be Excited About the Future

The future is exciting to visualize, isn't it? I'm sure you can see yourself laying on the beach in Jamaica right? I'm sure you booked in advance the beachside villa, shopped for the perfect swimsuits, purchased your plane tickets, put in your vacation time at your workplace, booked excursions for your visit, changed your currency, packed your bags, hired a house sitter, needless to say, you prepared. That's what being excited about the future is all about. It's preparing and in your prep being thrilled in knowing that something amazing is about to happen. You may not see it now but your future is the result of everything that you are doing right now and if you're doing the right things, what's not to be excited about. This isn't to say that all things must be perfect. We will make mistakes and yes, these mistakes will prepare us for the future. I know I said that we are finished but I want to do one more fun activity with you as a bonus. I want you to list all the things that you are looking forward to in the future. This will be two lists. One list will focus on the intangible and the other will focus on the tangible. Make it fun and make it exciting. If you have a magazine lets create a mini vision board that coincides with that list of items on the pages following the exercise. This will make certain that your wants and needs are always at the top of your mind so that you know exactly what you are fighting for. This is your vision, so make it good and if things change down the road, that's alright. Take a moment to ask yourself why did this change and if it is for a legitimate reason and you're not just giving up, I say go ahead and change it out. If you aren't excited about your future who will?

We will encounter many circumstances in our lives that move us to take action in our lives. For you to open your mind and realize the truth, sometimes life gives us a little push to do what we are supposed to be doing. It completely shifts our mind into a mindset that wakes you up to your true reason for existing or it would make you start the actual self-search to discover what you were meant to contribute to this world. In 2014, I was living in a small studio apartment. I lived alone and didn't have visitors over and was working long hours at the night shift so my social life was 90% evaporated. I had just been promoted in the company and wanted to see that I was on the path to be promoted again soon. So I practically gave up a lot of myself although I was headed down a miserable job path. To be honest, I truly believed that the next position would be better and I would be happy. One day while I was at home, I had begun boiling water to help with purification. I had done this before so I thought I was ok. Oh, how I was wrong. As soon as the water reached the boiling point, I immediately took the pot off the burner and began to pour it into the water pitcher. The water pitcher was made of thick glass and was pretty heavy duty. (I'm sure you can kind of guess where this is going). As I am pouring the boiling hot water into the glass pitcher, the entire pitcher shattered into thick pieces. All the water and the thick pieces of glass fell to the floor. With it happening so fast and unable to catch my balance, I slipped, fell to the ground. I was burned by the water and thankfully I dodged falling on the glass pieces otherwise it definitely would have either killed or seriously injured me. (I purchased the pitcher from Target, so you know it was a good quality glass. Just saying). I am uncertain how I missed falling on the glass pieces and not sure why I decided to pour boiling hot water into it, but that moment in my life freaked me out completely. I was alone and no one would have been able to help me. My mom is dead, my father was absent and absent-minded. I could have died. That was a wake-up call for me to reclaim the life I wanted regardless of the turmoil that I was faced with. I began to build the life that I wanted for myself and my future family. Now there would be other wake up calls along this journey as well however this one prompted it all. I am uncertain what wake up call you have been ignoring but I ask you to answer it. The world needs your full self. Let that be your new beginning in life. Everyone wants and deserves a do-over. You might not be able to start from a physical beginning such as being a baby, but you can have a rebirth into society. Celebrities do it all the time. So take after them if you are still skeptical.

Who we are is found in our grief. Not at the "end" of it once we are "over it." I'm not saying that you need to force yourself to be sad and lonely to activate your true self. What that means is that you will need to understand that you will feel those emotions and will go through a variety of them. However, you will need to have the ability to control it and redirect the emotions. For example, when you are feeling lonely transition to believing that your loved one is still with you and refer to chapter four on what family times means in your life. You will need to trust your heart and smile knowing that it is the truth. Another option is to transition that thought into knowing that the life that they lived was fulfilled with love, joy and purpose. Channel it into knowing that they have made an impression upon you and everyone around them that will last a lifetime. If you are feeling saddened, begin to ask yourself a few questions so that you may regain yourself. Ask, Why am I feeling sad right now? What am I currently doing that is making me feel this way? Am I looking at pictures for an extended amount of time that I now don't know how to return to reality? What can I do at this moment to cherish their death? Can I journal? Would I be better if I reached out to a sibling or fellow associate just to chat about the loss? You love this person and it's sad to see them go. That is a natural reaction, but tips like these will allow you to gather the strength in yourself time after time and soon enough you will see just how resilient and courageous you can be in your vulnerability. Your emotional maturity will skyrocket. Take it easy on yourself and begin to create your "go-to" list of things to help you move forward in your grief. There isn't such a thing as "I'm over it" when it comes to losing a loved one. That only means that you have no intention of remembering your loved one and have possibly decided to suppress everything that you are feeling as a safeguard. We must learn to live on each day facing it head-on as it will get better with time.

Losing a loved one, as we know it, is quite alarming and sometimes sporadic. Down to the very second, no one knows when it is set to strike. My goal for writing this book is solely for survivors. This was written with every person who has lost a loved one, in mind. Yes, for you. Those remaining to grieve often find themselves left to pick up the pieces of a shattered heart, soul and mind. Leaving a lot of things up in the air. Your loved ones are important and you know who else is important? Those left behind. You must acknowledge that life will keep moving and you must jump on board. Death = Dear Earthly Animals, Take Heed. It's a clear warning to take your life back and keep moving. What do you take heed to, you ask? Everything. You must live each day knowing that you gave it your all, knowing that you are alive and that you must fulfill your purpose. It means you must live, just live. It's going to be ok. There is no need to go through the day worrying yourself sick. Worrying only makes things worse. Test question. Name one incident where worrying solved the world's problems? I'm sure you can't think of a single episode. It's a trap to worry. It builds a wall of anxiety and uncertainty that seems unbreakable.

However, there are a couple of things that you can do to help ease the situation and begin to "take heed" in life. That is through first, showing gratitude. This shouldn't come as a shocker. I am certain that each of you was taught to say "thank you" as early as you could talk. Your mom and dad were right, after all, go figure. This teaches and reminds us that we are better off than we might think. This also helps us to acknowledge all the good that is happening in our lives and all the wonderful gifts that life has given us. If you are having a hard time finding something to be thankful for, start by looking in the mirror and choose at least one to two things that you like about yourself and write them down. If you find more, I want you to write them down as well. I can help you with the first thing. If you are looking in the mirror, be grateful that you can see as in retrospect, someone may not be able to see at all. This may seem small but that is grand for some people. Once you start to recognize the "small" things that you are so privileged to have and experience, you will then be able to open your mind a bit more to appreciate life and the people around you.

The next that will help is to laugh. I'm talking laugh like you just left a comedy show featuring your favorite comedian where you almost soiled your pants or your eyes started leaking (crying laughing and you turned red in the face with almost no air left to breathe). You could barely talk. Give it your all and don't take everything so seriously. Loosen your tie, or hair tie, and relax into yourself. At some point in our lives, we stopped laughing. It could be when your rent payment was due along with your car note and having to feed the family while paying the utilities, taking out the dog, going to work for 8-15 hours each day, paying the insurance, paying off debt, whew! When do we get a break? I know I'm not alone here (at least I hope I'm not). It's exhausting and quite frankly there's nothing to laugh about when it comes to a life where it's hard to find the joke. We must find a good laugh somewhere. Search for it and make it intentional. What I want you to do is ask yourself, "When was the last time I laughed?" What was the scenario and why was it so funny? I hope that moment made you smile if not giggle just a little bit. We only live one life and letting ourselves have the freedom to laugh lets a light shine through in such a much needed time. The last thing is to lead a life with passion. A true-life of passion will lead you to love again and live with enthusiasm. This type of strong emotion can push you day by day with a strong feeling of desire. The desire to be you and grow into a you that you wouldn't recognize in 10 years. It's a desire to be free to execute your heart's passion. Passion is led by your heart's desire. Be convicted about your choices and stand strong and firm in them. This is what will move you to make a, "for the better," change. Let this be the beginning of your new life. I am excited for you, so congratulations. Congratulations on being willing to take your healing to the next step. Wow, You've made it so far. Can you believe it?

DEBUNKING MYTHS SURROUNDING GRIEF

We are surrounded by plenty of people with plenty of ideas on how you should handle and cope with your grief. If we are honest with ourselves, some of them can be either offensive or far reached for someone who has to try and understand what you're going through. Sometimes we create answers in our head based on what our parents have displayed or have told us indirectly and western culture doesn't make it easy for us to grieve. Regardless, we are filled consistently with different stances of mourning and grief. I want to share with you some of the most common myths that I have encountered in my lifetime and expose the falseness in each of them. Let's start with the most common:

1. There is a time limit attached to when you should be completely done grieving:

I am sure you have heard this in some form or fashion. "You're still Grieving? You should have been done grieving a while ago." You may have placed a timeline on yourself. "I should be done grieving in six months" or after a year is up you ask yourself, "Why am I still grieving or crying over them." This is unrealistic. There is no specific timeline of "getting over" the death of your loved one. It will take time. If you have people around you that seem to be putting pressure on you to so-called "complete the grieving process" you will need to remind them that their support during this time would be much appreciated and if they aren't emotionally available for that type of support that they should allow their opinions to remain within themselves. Do not rush yourself and please do not allow others to rush you. Point out to me the law that says that you must be done by a certain time? Why is it an issue if you are taking "too long?" When we begin putting time constraints on our feelings we will find ourselves back at square one.

2. Children won't understand losing a loved one and do not grieve/ they shouldn't go to funerals:

Children are perhaps the freest yet sensitive beings on the planet in my opinion. They are completely vulnerable to what is happening around them. When it comes to grief know that children are very observant. Seeing grandpa every day to not see him the next or waking up every morning to say good morning and having a blast with one of their siblings, to no longer having their favorite playmate; children notice and as the adult you will need to explain what turn of event happened in their life. Without a doubt, they will have questions. Children will react differently to the way you would react as an adult. Their behaviors may and will possibly take a vow of silence. Children feel and experience all emotions just as we adults feel and experience. Adults display anger, sadness, or even happiness differently from one another. Some are giddy with excitement and others are a bit more composed with their happiness. So we shouldn't expect children to display zero emotion when it comes to grief. Children grieve as well and in addition to that, you must welcome them to the funeral and perhaps explain what they can expect by attending. This is a vital part of their future self-learning to live with their loss. They will need to say goodbye just like you. Remember chapter three "I too grieve dad"

3. There is a "right way" to grieve or if you're not following the stages of grief you are doing it wrong.

You've probably searched the internet for "stages of grief" during your time of healing. You read it and found that you either skipped over a step, isn't following the steps at all, or is right on track with the stages. It can be quite stressful when it comes to dealing with your grief only to find out that you are "doing it wrong." You must take steps to deal with it healthily but people grieve differently and for some, it doesn't hit them at the time of death. Crying doesn't mean you are doing it right or wrong. You must figure out what works for you and be open to different concepts of grief management. Let me remind you that it must be done healthily. Getting to the bottom of a bottle to feel good at that moment, isn't dealing with it. It's temporary relief (or is it?). You have to find ways that confront the issue head-on while you walk through your fear. No matter what, understand that this is your journey where you will run into some road bumps. However, you must continue. Do not get caught and stuck on "the right way" to do something. Start and keep moving. You will thank yourself later.

4. To move past grief, you must get rid of all of their belongings:

We went over this in chapter four and if you want a deeper look, review the section of "show and Tell." This is a fallacy in everyday life and is proven to be counterproductive to your healing process. The idea that "everything" must go is horrendous and should not be practiced. There is a spectrum that you must adhere to when it involves your deceased loved one belongings. You don't want to hoard but you also don't want to extract everything. It's not the "material things" that delay the healing process, however, it is the unhealthy attachment and strong connection that the items have on you. It is a combination of your emotional attachment to things as well. As I have mentioned, you should reference chapter four for a deeper understanding.

5. It's "just" a dog! (or a cat, horse, gerbil, hamster, ferret, rabbit, etc...pet):

This is one of my favorites that I have heard that makes me chuckle a little bit and although I have not gone into detail on this subject in this book, please know that this is not an accurate statement. Humans very well grieve when it comes to the death of the family pet. Notice I said "family pet." This is the case for pets as they are a part of the family. Some pets are with families for long periods. The average dog can live up to 15 years, the average cat can live up to 16 years and a horse can very well live up to 30 years so these are not "just animals." They were a vital part of your life and in many cases have been lifesavers for their humans. Feel free to shed a tear for your furry friend and mourn their death.

JOURNAL ACTIONS

So you've lost your loved one and are having a hard time picking up the pieces. You must be at a loss for words. After all, you never thought something like death would happen to you. It's so close to home. It's meant for others, right? You thought you had the time and unfortunately, the time has run out. You've fought at your emotions long enough and your grief is too overwhelming so you begin to question life. Should I cry or shouldn't I? Why am I sinking? Is this quicksand where I'm standing? It seems that every time I want out of this pit it brings me back down. The more I fight it, the worse I feel. Can someone please pull me out of here? I need a lifeline, please. Millions of people die each year, leaving millions of people to their pain. Leaving millions of people to suffer in silence suppressing the very feelings that are birthed as a result of their death, out of "reverence" of the dead. At what cost? Your sanity, your peace, your livelihood, your health? You are lost and confused. Your parents are lost and confused. Your friends are inadvertently insensitive. Everyone affected seems to be doing ok, so they too are ignoring the fact that a huge piece of their lives was just taken from them. Making your grief insignificant which forces you to fight alone and put your mask on just like everyone else. Are the others suffering too? Did they love them as much as you did? How is it that you're the only one that can't stop thinking about your deceased loved one? It's a lot to handle and here's where the good news comes. You can have freedom in your grief.

These journal entries were created with you in mind. Journaling is a helpful task in helping individuals understand how they feel to move forward. Sort of like an antidote. This is one of many ways of expression. This is your opportunity to release all that you have been holding on to. Take each exercise seriously. You may follow along while you read the book or you may decide that you want to participate after you have read the whole book. Give yourself permission to go all in and leave nothing. Again I hope that you begin to realize the freedom that is found in your grief.

SOMETHING MORE TO GET STARTED: THE WORKOUT, THE MEAL, AND BEYOND

Exercising can help you feel happier, lose weight, gain more energy, assist in fighting diseases among many other benefits. For some, getting started can be tiresome and they may or may not know where to begin. Especially if they have never gone to the gym or participated in any sports. How often should I work out? What do I do once I get to the gym? There are so many machines, am I supposed to automatically know how to use them? I think I just want to start off with bodyweight exercise, besides I can barely lift 10 lbs. (which you likely can't hold a small child).

Below I have written a sample workout plan with descriptive information for you to follow and maintain for about three months until it's time to switch up the routine. Before you get started let's go over a few things.

1. These exercises may be conducted in your home, the park or in a gym setting.

2. The notes and exercises are going to be beginner style information

3. Make sure to have plenty of water available but not too much. The purpose is to keep you hydrated.

4. Have a towel, or not if you like to feel the sweat (sometimes your sweat can be a motivator).

5. Never exercise on a full stomach or an empty one.

6. You will need one set of dumbbells at a challenging weight. Or feel free to find two plastic water jugs that you have emptied and filled with sand at a comfortable weight

7. Know your limits but push your limits. Just when you feel like you did your last one, push for one more.

8. When trying a new exercise start with light weight, and practice your form.

9. Completing exercises with Proper form is everything. Never compromise your form for lifting heavy weight.

10. If you have any injuries or medical conditions, these exercises are not to replace your medications or "heal" you. You will need to consult your physician.

11. Set a specific goal for yourself, and once you meet it, set another and so forth.

12. Be consistent. Set time for your exercises daily, and be committed to your goals

13. Remember, everyone has to start somewhere.

14. Set a timer, workouts below are meant to last no longer than 35 minutes.

15. Words to understand: Set- consists of X amount of a singular exercise in a row. Repetitions are the number of times you complete a single exercise before taking a rest or a break EX: 3 sets of 12. This means that the same movement 12 times before you take a break and do it again for a total of three times.

16. Last but not least, play your favorite music on your TV, speakers, phone, etc. let's get you going.

Warm up Options (choose one of the options, and feel free to switch up daily)

Jump Rope for 5-10 Mins

Jumping Jacks for 5-10 minutes

10 minute run, either in place, around your apartment complex, around the neighborhood block, or on a piece of cardio equipment such as a treadmill.

2 sets of 10 pushups - Variations: Standing wall pushups, Floor pushup on knees, full push up from toes

Monday Wednesday, Friday Exercises

Round 1

On these days we will work on the particular muscle groups: Biceps, Triceps, Legs,

Standing bicep curls:

Stand with a weight in each hand, arms by your side. Face palms forward. Begin to raise your hand wrist and forearm slowly attempting to reach the top of your shoulder while squeezing your actual bicep.Return to starting position, and that's one rep. Do this, 6-8 times, either alternating each arm or simultaneously. (about 25 secs active, and 5 secs rest) Once you complete set 1 go right into the next exercise of Tricep Dips.

Tricep Dips:

Begin by sitting on the edge of your sofa, chair, stool, etc with both hands placed on the edge. With your legs straight out before you, heel of your feet on the ground lift yourself and slowly walk your legs out further until your arms are behind you at an angle. At this point you are ready to "dip"you but in the empty air beneath it. Keeping a staring forearm and dip as low to create a 90 degree angle in the crease of your elbow. Be sure to squeeze your triceps on the way up. Do this 6-8 times. (about 25 secs active, and 5 secs rest) Next:

Body Weight Squats:

Using either one weight or none, start by standing with both feet apart, about shoulder width, if you have longer legs you should go out further. Keeping you chest squared and forward, back straight (no curving). Squat down as if you were about to sit on a chair, but then you changed your mind to get back up to the starting position. You want to shoot for a minimum 90 degree angle bend in your knee. Do as many as you can at a comfortable pace for 50 sec active and 10 secs rest .

After you finish the body weight squats, Start from the beginning of the round. You will do this round three times before you deserve a long break of 30 seconds. This will give you time to catch your breath and or get a drink of water.

Round two

Seated Dumbbell concentration Curls:

Sit on a flat bench with your legs spread, knees bent and your feet flat on the floor with a dumbbell between your feet.

Use either arm to pick the dumbbell up and hold it with an underhand grip.

Place the back of that upper arm on the top of your inner thigh on the same side. Your palm should be facing away from your thigh.

Keep your arm fully extended downwards without letting the dumbbell rest on the floor. This is the start position.

Curl the dumbbell forward and up in a smooth arc, contracting your biceps and exhaling.

Continue curling the dumbbell upward until your biceps are fully contracted and the dumbbell is at shoulder level. Hold for a count of one while squeezing your biceps.

Return to the start position in a controlled, smooth arc inhaling as you do so. Do not swing the dumbbell down.

Repeat for all the repetitions for that arm then switch and repeat the movement with your other arm.

Do 6-8 reps. (about 25 secs active, and 5 secs rest)

Overhead Tricep Extension:
With feet shoulder-width apart and core tight, hold a dumbbell with both hands

Lift the dumbbell until your arms are fully extended with palms facing the roof and elbows pointing forward. This is the start position

Bending at the elbows and squeezing your triceps, slowly lower the dumbbell behind your head

Slowly return to start position and repeat

Do 6-8 Reps. (about 25 secs active, and 5 secs rest)

Jumping lunges:
Stand with feet shoulder-width apart, with your core engaged.

Take a big step forward with your right leg. Keep your arms by your side.

Shift your weight forward with this leg, so your heel touches the floor first. Then lower your body until the forward leg is parallel to the floor. This is the bottom position.

Jump up, quickly switching the position of your feet while mid-air so your right leg moves back behind you and your left leg comes forward. To help you move explosively, propel your arms into the air while you jump.

Gently land back on the floor in a basic lunge position with the opposite leg forward.

Repeat this movement pattern, switching legs on each jump, for the desired amount of time or repetitions. Beginners should aim for 5 to 10 reps on each leg or 30 seconds total. As this gets easier, work your way up to 60 seconds of continuous jumping lunges.

After you finish the jumping lunges, Start from the beginning of the round. You will do this round three times before you deserve a long break of 30 seconds. This will give you time to catch your breath and or get a drink of water.

Round 3

One-Arm Dumbbell Row:

You need a bench or a sturdy thigh-high platform to lean on when doing the exercise, so secure that first and place a dumbbell on the floor to one side of it. Put your left leg on the bench and grab the far side with your left hand, then bend over so your upper body is parallel with the ground. Reach down and pick up the dumbbell in your right hand with a neutral grip (palm facing you), then hold it with your arm extended, keeping your back straight.

Bring the dumbbell up to your chest, concentrating on lifting it with your back and shoulder muscles rather than your arms. Keep your chest still as you lift. At the top of the movement, squeeze your shoulder and back muscles. Lower the dumbbell slowly until your arm is fully extended again. Do all your reps on one arm before switching to the other side

Do 6-8 reps. (about 25 secs active, and 5 secs rest)

Lying Skull Crushers:

Lie flat on the bench or floor with a dumbbell in each hand (or a weighted barbell with both hands). Make sure you head is near the edge of the bench.

Carefully extend your arms so the weight is above your head.

Bending at the elbows slowly lower the dumbbells towards your shoulders and pause

The return to start position and repeat.

Do 6-8 reps. (about 25 secs active, and 5 secs rest)

Standing Calf Raises:

Starting Position - Stand 6 -12" away from a wall with your feet hip-width apart and facing forward. Extend your arms to place your palms on the wall, level with your chest or shoulders.

Upward Phase - Exhale and slowly lift your heels off the floor keeping your knees extended and without rotating your feet. Use your hands on the wall to support your body. Hold your raised position briefly.

Downward Phase - Inhale and slowly lower your heels back towards the floor.

Do this for about 50 seconds

After you finish the Standing Calf Raises, Start from the beginning of the round. You will do this round three times before you deserve a long break of 30 seconds. This will give you time to catch your breath and or get a drink of water.

Tuesday, Thursday, Saturday Exercises

On these days we will work on the particular muscle groups: Chest (Pectoralis), Back (Latissimus Dorsi), Shoulders (Deltoids)

Round 1

Incline pushups:

The basic incline pushup is done using a bench, table, or another solid surface that is about 3 feet high. Here's how to do this style correctly:

Stand facing the bench, table, or the edge of a bed.

Place your hands on the edge of the bench just slightly wider than shoulder width. Your arms are straight but elbows are not locked. Align your feet so that your arms and body are completely straight.

Bend your elbows to slowly lower your chest to the edge of the bench while inhaling. Keep your body straight and rigid throughout the movement.

Push your body away from the bench until your elbows are extended, but not locked. Exhale as you push up.

Keep going with slow, steady repetitions.

Do 6-8 reps. (about 25 secs active, and 5 secs rest

Dumbbell Bent over Row:
Stand with legs about shoulder-width apart, with knees soft or slightly bent. Hold a dumbbell in each hand, palms facing the body, holding them shoulder-width apart.

With a dumbbell in each hand, bend over at about a 45-degree angle (no farther). Keep the back straight throughout the exercise. Brace your abdominals and breathe in.

Lift the weights straight up, exhaling. While lifting, the arms should go no higher than parallel with the shoulders—slightly lower than the shoulders is fine. While lifting, try to keep the wrists from excessive extra movement down or to the side. Do not squat down and up after the initial pose. No movement of the legs occurs throughout the exercise.

Lower the weights in a controlled manner while inhaling.

Remain bent over until all repetitions are complete.

Do 6-8 reps. (about 25 secs active, and 5 secs rest)

Shoulder shrugs:

Start by standing on your two feet holding a weight in each hand. Arms by your side. Move your shoulder up and down leaving your arms by your side to say "I don't know." Be sure to squeeze your deltoids. Do this for about 50 seconds.

After you finish the Shoulder Shrugs, Start from the beginning of the round. You will do this round three times before you deserve a long break of 30 seconds. This will give you time to catch your breath and or get a drink of water.

Round 2

Seated Inner Chest Press:

Starting Position: Sit with your back firmly supported against a backrest. Grip one dumbbell with both hands and raise it level to your mid-chest (at the nipple line). Position your feet firmly on the floor or on the foot rests to stabilize your body. Stiffen ("brace") your abdominal muscles to stabilize your spine, but do not press your low back into the backrest. Maintain the natural arch in your low back and avoid arching your back throughout the exercise. Depress and retract your scapulae (pull shoulders back and down) and attempt to hold this position throughout the exercise.

Gently exhale and slowly perform a pressing movement, extending both your arms in front, while maintaining a neutral wrist position, and keep your head aligned with your spine while avoiding any arching of your low back.

Continue pressing until your elbows are fully extended, but not locked. Your shoulder blades should continue to make contact with the backrest and not round or bend forward. Pause momentarily then gently allow your elbows to flex (bend) in a slow, controlled manner while returning the bar back towards the starting position. Repeat the movement 10 -15 times. About 30 secs.

Military Shoulder Press:
Grab two dumbbells and sit on an incline bench. Make sure the back of the bench is set at a 90-degree angle.

Once you're seated, rest one dumbbell on each thigh. Sit with your lower back firmly against the back of the bench. Keep your shoulders and back as straight as possible.

Raise the dumbbells from your thighs and bring them to shoulder height. If you have heavy dumbbells, raise your thighs one at a time to help lift the dumbbells. Raising a heavy dumbbell with only your arm could cause injury.

With the dumbbells at shoulder height, rotate your palms so that they face forward. If you prefer, you can also complete a dumbbell press with your palms facing your body. Make sure your forearms are perpendicular to the ground.

Begin to press the dumbbells above your head until your arms fully extend. Hold the weight above your head for a moment, and then lower the dumbbells back to shoulder height.

Complete the desired number of reps. If you're a beginner, start with 1 set of 8–10 reps. (about 25 secs active, and 5 secs rest)

Supermans:
Lie on your belly, with your arms and legs fully extended.

Lift both arms and legs off the floor, and hold for a count of 2.

Return to the starting position and repeat.

If you're a beginner, start with 1 set of 8–10 reps. (about 25 secs active, and 5 secs rest)

After you finish the Supermans, Start from the beginning of the round. You will do this round three times before you deserve a long break of 30 seconds. This will give you time to catch your breath and or get a drink of water.

Round 3

Regular pushups:
Get down on all fours, placing your hands slightly wider than your shoulders.

Straighten your arms and legs.

Lower your body until your chest nearly touches the floor.

Pause, then push yourself back up.

Repeat 10 times about 25 secs

Reverse Fly:
Holding a dumbbell in each hand, hinge forward at the waist until your torso forms a 45-degree angle

with the ground, allowing the dumbbells to hang in front of you, palms facing each other. Have a slight bend in your elbows.

Engaging your core, lift your arms up and out, squeezing your shoulder blades at the top.

Slowly return to the starting position, staying in control of the weights. Complete 3 sets of 12 reps

Single Arm Lateral Raise:
Position dumbbell in front of pelvis with elbow slightly bent. Grasp stationary object with other hand for support. Bend over with hips and knees bent slightly.

Raise upper arm to side until elbow is shoulder height. Maintain elbow's height above or equal to wrist. Lower and repeat. Continue with the opposite arm.

If you're a beginner, start with 1 set of 8–10 reps. (about 25 secs active, and 5 secs rest)

After you finish the single arm lateral raise,, Start from the beginning of the round. You will do this round three times before you deserve a long break of 30 seconds. This will give you time to catch your breath and or get a drink of water.

The Meals: Tips that will aid in your complete wellness Journey

1. The foods you eat will determine if you see results or not

2. Do not starve yourself

3. Always keep hydrated with water.

4. You can find plenty of water in your fruits and vegetables. Be sure to load up on those.

5. Refrain from consuming sugary drinks and treats.

6. Allow yourself a "treat day" but don't over do it all of your hard work will disappear.

7. Have a nutritious meal following your workout.

8. Prepare meals in advance. This will help you save and refrain from eating splurging on unhealthy eats.

9. You will need discipline.

10. Remember your goals and keep them at the forefront of your decisions.

11. Get the whole family involved. There's nothing like watching your partner and kids gobble down a whole box of pizza while you are on a diet change.

12. Diet does not mean that you should only consume salads. Have fun with your meals. Make it exciting. Instead of cooking with butter, use grapeseed oil or olive oil, Find healthy substitutions and enjoy your meals.

13. Be patient. Weighing yourself everyday will be depressing. Stop watching the scale and watch the foods you eat and your workouts.

14. Take pictures of yourself at different angles with a relaxed body at the beginning of your journey and every two weeks or 30 days (preferably 30 days). Front, back and sides. You have the option to be clothless (just your undergarments) or not. Remember these pictures are just for you and not anyone else so guard them.

One of my Favorite Vegan Recipes

Rigatoni with Roasted Tomatoes and Arugula

Serves: 4
Prep Time: 15 Minutes
Cook Time: 20 Minutes

Ingredients:

1 pint Cherry Tomatoes
3 Shallots, Thinly Sliced
Sea Salt (or regular)
Freshly Ground Black Pepper
3 Tablespoons Extra Virgin Olive Oil
One 9 ounce box Rigatoni Pasta
3 Cloves Garlic, Minced

3 Tablespoons Red Wine Vinegar

4 Ounces Green Olives Halved

¼ teaspoon Red Pepper Flakes

2 Cups Baby Arugula

1. Preheat the oven to 400F.

2. Bring a large pot of water to boil over high heat.

3. In a large ovenproof saute pan, place cherry tomatoes and shallots in a single layer. Season to taste with sea salt and black pepper and drizzle with olive oil. Put the pan in the preheated oven and cook for 20 minutes, until the tomatoes and shallots are soft.

4. Meanwhile, add the rigatoni to the boiling water. Cook according to the package directions, until the pasta is al dente, nine to 12 minutes. Drain the pasta.

5. When the tomatoes and shallots are done roasting, move the pan to the stovetop and turn the stove on medium-high. Be careful not to touch the handle of the pan without a potholder.

6. Add garlic to the pan and cook, stirring constantly, until it is fragrant, about 30 seconds.

7. Add the red wine vinegar and olives to the pan, using the side of the spoon to scrape any browned bits from the

bottom of the pan. Bring to a simmer and stir in the red pepper flakes.

8. Toss the vegetables with pasta, stirring in the arugula, which will wilt slightly from heat. Serve immediately.

You may store pasta in the refrigerator for up to one week without the arugula mixed in.

ACKNOWLEDGEMENTS

Wow, what a journey this has been. my heart, mind and soul are forever indebted to you God. Thank you for being patient and kind to me even when I wasn't to myself. You are for me and not against me and will continue to do great work in me until completion. My prayer is that everyone who reads this book will know you and be comforted by you. Let your love reach them as it has reached me. To my twin sister, Meagan Hale, I love you dearly. Thank you so much to you and your team, for endlessly editing and proofreading copy with me. You have no clue how you inspire me each day and how grateful I am for you. Your encouragement along the way was needed and I thank you. We had a long walk home, but I'm glad it was with you. You are intelligent, beautiful and a great mother & wife. Continue being strong and yet vulnerable. My heart is with you forever. There is nothing that can break the bond that we have. To Peay, although it was a brief moment you spent with me, I thank you for your words "Never deny your mother." My eyes were opened. To my mother Gail, although I never knew you, I know your love stood powerfully encamped around me. Protecting me, guiding me and going to war for me. Thank you for showing yourself to me in the times where I needed you the most. To Justice, my youngest brother from a different mother, I think about you often. You are smart and truly meant to do amazing things. I charge you to be brave and never give up for you will always be one step closer to victory. Everything you need is within you, so there is no need to look anywhere else. To my siblings, life has been rough, I know. On July 30, 2014, at 3:45 am, I wrote a letter to you all that came pouring from my heart:

Family,

Everything that God created and has done, has a purpose here on this earth. Chairs for sitting, food for eating...etc, and who are we as God's children to be placed on this earth and he not give a purpose? Each one of us was born with a mission attached to our name, and it's up to you to accomplish that goal. We are here on this earth with reason, and in particular, I believe that God has placed a mark on this family, in which devils have tried so hard to remove. From the death of one mom to the installation of another, from the tragedy of one dad to the mistake of another, we still stand with guards all around us. When I think of you I think of how amazing I know each one of you can be, but you have to believe in how amazing you can be. Every negative force, every negative feeling, every stronghold that has been placed on your life, and in your life, has NO POWER unless you give it power! No one is to blame but yourself for the abundance or lack thereof. If you want more, go after it! Let no one stop you! It has already been predestined by God for you to have it, so why limit yourself. REMOVE THE LIMITS. FOR THERE ARE NO LIMITS WITH GOD. In all be patient, and be willing to work for it. Gods not going to just drop it out of the sky and place it right in your hands, of course, he has the power to do so. I declare life to the things that were once dead...every dream, every vision, every plan. But you have to believe and declare it as well. Allow The Lord to be your confidence and your strength. I believe in you guys, and am excited about what this family is going to accomplish and set precedence, and set standards for men and women everywhere! I am extremely proud to be a member of the Hale Family. I love each of you with all of my beings and I pray God's freedom, love, and prosperity in and over your lives.

CALL TO ACTION

Before you go: I want to take the time to say, Thank you! To you, the reader. Now that you have reached the end, I am asking you specifically to take one more step and that is to leave a review on the web page from whence you purchased, ie Amazon or Audible, Barnes and Noble, etc. This is the best way for independent authors and authors with small publishers to gain exposure to reach more people and help sales. Again, I thank you for the time that we have spent together as this would not be possible without you.

Citations and References

Abpp, P. W. W. J. (2018). Grief Counseling and Grief Therapy, Fifth Edition: A Handbook for the Mental Health Practitioner – Grief Counseling Handbook on Treatment of Grief, Loss and Bereavement, Book and Free eBook (5th ed.). Springer Publishing Company.

Facc, M. N. B. D. (2018). The Vegan Starter Kit: Everything You Need to Know About Plant-Based Eating (1st ed.). Grand Central Publishing.

Kastenbaum, R., & Moreman, C. M. (2018). Death, Society, and Human Experience (12th ed.). Routledge.

Shasta Press, & Nelson-Bunge, T. A. (2014). Vegan Recipes in 30 Minutes: A Vegan Cookbook with 106 Quick & Easy Recipes (Reprint ed.). Shasta Press.

Trozzi, M. (1999). Talking with Children About Loss: Words, Strategies, and Wisdom to Help Children Cope with Death, Divorce, and (1st ed.). TarcherPerigee.

Website references

https://www.healthline.com/health/jumping-lunges

https://www.acefitness.org/education-and-resources/lifestyle/exercise-library/73/standing-calf-raises-wall/

https://workoutlabs.com/exercise-guide/concentration-curls/

https://www.puregym.com/exercises/arms-and-shoulders/tricep-extension/

https://www.coachmag.co.uk/dumbbell-exercises/7380/how-to-do-the-one-arm-dumbbell-row

https://www.verywellfit.com/incline-push-up-for-beginners-3120038

https://www.healthline.com/health/dumbbell-military-press#seated

https://www.acefitness.org/education-and-resources/lifestyle/exercise-library/188/seated-chest-press/

https://www.healthline.com/health/fitness/back-strengthening-muscles-posture#24

https://www.exrx.net/WeightExercises/DeltoidLateral/DBOneArmLateralRaise

https://www.cdc.gov/nchs/fastats/deaths.htm

http://www.us-funerals.com/funeral-articles/cheap-funeral.html#.Xqer6iVOmEc

https://couplestherapyinc.com/honeymoon-phase-wears-off/

https://www.google.com/amp/s/www.psychologytoday.com/us/blog/evil-deeds/201202/dsm-5-hysteria-when-normal-mourning-becomes-neurotic-bereavement%3famp

https://takelessons.com/live/singing/health-benefits-of-singing